Modern Poetry in T

Series 3 / N

Metamorphoses

Edited by David and Helen Constantine

Modern Poetry in Translation No. 3
Series Three
© Modern Poetry in Translation 2005 and contributors
ISBN 0-9545367-3-8
ISSN 0969-3572
Typeset by Paul Dunn
Printed and bound in Great Britain by Short Run Press, Exeter

Editors: David and Helen Constantine
Reviews Editor: Josephine Balmer
Administrator: Deborah de Kock

Submissions should be sent in hard copy with return postage to David
and Helen Constantine, Queen's College, Oxford, OX1 4AW, UK.
Unless agreed in advance, submissions by email will not be considered.
Translators are themselves responsible for obtaining any necessary per-
missions and copyright clearance.

Founding Editors:
Ted Hughes and Daniel Weissbort

Subscription Rates: see page 152

Modern Poetry in Translation is represented in UK by Central Books
99 Wallis Road, London, E9 5LN

For orders: tel +44 (0) 845 458 9910 Fax +44 (0) 845 458 9912
or visit www.mptmagazine.com

Contents

5 **Editorial** David and Helen Constantine

Akhmatova on the South Bank

9 **Ruth Borthwick** Anna of all the Russias: Translating Akhmatova
00 **Elaine Feinstein** An Evening for Akhmatova
15 **Colette Bryce** Six poems
17 **Sasha Dugdale** Five poems
23 **Jo Shapcott** Five poems
27 **George Szirtes** (with Veronika Krasnova) Six poems
31 **Marilyn Hacker** 'For Anna Akhmatova'

35 **John Greening** 'Coming Soon. *Remastered from the Old Norse*'
41 **Neil Philip** '21 glosses on poems from *The Greek Anthology*'
48 **Paul Howard** Versions of four sonnets by Giuseppe Belli
53 **Terence Dooley** A version of Raymond Queneau's 'La Pendule'
57 **Kathleen Jamie** Hölderlin into Scots. Two poems

60 **Josephine Balmer** *The Word for Sorrow*: a work begins its progress

Ingeborg Bachmann

69 **Karen Leeder** Introduction
72 **Mike Lyons** 'War Diary'
81 **Patrick Drysdale and Mike Lyons** Five Bachmann poems

86 **Sean O'Brien** A version of Canto V of Dante's *Inferno*
91 **Cristina Viti** Eros Alesi's *Fragments*
98 **Sarah Lawson and Malgorzata Koraszweska** Six poems by Anna Kühn-Cichocka
103 **Marilyn Hacker** Guy Goffette's 'Construction Site of the Elegy'
111 **Belinda Cooke and Richard McKane** Six poems by Boris Poplavsky
119 **Cecilia Rossi** Poems from Alejandra Pizarnik's *Works and Nights*
128 **Terence Cave** A memorial note on Edith McMorran and a translation of Aragon's 'C'

131 **Paul Batchelor** An essay on Barry MacSweeney's Apollinaire

Reviews

137 **Antony Wood** on Angela Livingstone's *Poems from Chevengur*
139 **Josephine Balmer** on Cliff Ashcroft's *Dreaming of Still Water* and Peter Boyle's Eugenio Montejo

141 **Paschalis Nikolaou** on Philip Ramp's Karouzos

143 **Francis Jones** on Jan Twardowski (translated by Sarah Lawson and Malgorzata Koraszweska) and *A Fine Line: New Poetry from Central and Eastern Europe*

147 **Books Received**

148 **Acknowledgements**

148 **Notes on Contributors**

152 **Subscription rates**

153 **Back Issues**

EDITORIAL

ALL TRANSLATION is metamorphosis. Even 'mimetic' translators, seeking to reproduce the form of the original, will, even at their closest, only ever produce in their own language something analogous and roughly equivalent. Forms called the same work differently according to the language constituting them. The alexandrine line, for example, was imported from France (via the Netherlands) into Germany in the seventeenth century; but in its one hundred and fifty years or so of frequent usage there it never sounded anything like Racine. In German, a heavily accented language, the central cæsura all too often chops the line in half; which the German Baroque writers, tending to view the world in stark antitheses, readily exploited. English blank verse, in part because of the abundance of monosyllabic words available to its users, sounds and works very differently than it does in German, which, being an inflected language, has far fewer such units to play with. Poetic forms may be thought to pre-exist a language, to be there waiting to be filled by words; but those words, of course, actually constitute the form: they give it its peculiar sensuous shape

Words are shapes in themselves; and even if, in translation, we move across literally from 'Brot' to 'pain' to 'bread', the effective shape of each is quite different in each mother tongue. The shape of a word is the whole and ever-changing sensuous presence it grows into in its own language - which is to say, in its culture, in its way of life. So even moving across between the languages word for word, translators are, however literal or mimetic they may wish to be, transformers of shape.

But for a good part of this issue we have focussed on translations in which some radical and evident reshaping has been consciously undertaken. In two instances - John Greening's 'Coming Soon' and Neil Philip's '21 glosses on poems from *The Greek Anthology*' - the shift is out of a remote past into the forms, language, tones and concerns of modern life. In three others, Kathleen Jamie's Hölderlin, Paul Howard's Belli and Terence Dooley's Queneau, the shift is largely linguistic - into Scots, Yorkshire dialect, street argot: and the shock comes perhaps from our being forced to concede that we expect a standard English, and here meet instead an appropriate and effective deviation. In the versions of Akhmatova the translators move more or less far (some via the medium of literal renderings of the Russian) towards or actually into poems of their own. Marilyn Hacker's 'For Anna Akhmatova' is the furthest along that line. And Josephine Balmer's *The Word for Sorrow*, still in progress, sets together a classical poetry of exile (Ovid's) and a twentieth-century documentation of wars abroad, in their shared location: the coasts of the

Black Sea. That juxtapositioning (which is a shaping of the whole) lights up and defamiliarizes each era and its human fates.

Poems live on if they are lively enough; most translations aren't, and don't. Hölderlin wrote to his publisher Friedrich Wilmans late in 1803 apologizing that he had not yet delivered his Sophocles translations: their language, he said, was not yet lively enough. Metamorphosis is perhaps best understood as a way of staying alive. By its agility, by being able to shift and change, a translation makes a bid for longer life. The poem has this quality inbuilt, or it would not be a poem. The translation, bound one way or another and in greater or lesser degree to that vital original, has a harder job engendering the kindred vitality without which it will not live.

As we said in our first issue, by 'modern' in the name of this magazine we chiefly intend to signal a present liveliness. So we shall always be on the look-out for translations eluding death by changing shape. And this interest is very closely connected with our other staple topic: exile, the more or less enforced wandering abroad. Indeed, exile and metamorphosis do as a matter of fact have much in common. Languages on the move, the spirit of poetic utterance constantly on the move, constantly having to find itself new shapes... Do the writers thrust abroad still have a native tongue? One that will serve them for all they now must say? Must they transform that tongue? Or learn another, and transform it for their purposes?

This matters for the writers - they must move and change or die - and it matters for the readers too, who will settle comfortably into what is habitual, unless new things, or old things in new shapes, continually assail them. Changing appearances will help keep us in a living connection with things; they show us new facets, we view them from new perspectives. Translation - an act of changing shape - should be understood as partaking of an intention which is central in most poetics: to resist habituation, to unsettle, to awake and increase the reader's liveliness.

This issue of *MPT* is, we think, very rich and various, and these remarks on metamorphosis and on some present instances of it by no means cover the material that has come our way. We shan't ever be restricted by any particular concern, however large that may be. Given the chance - thanks to the generosity of Heinz Bachmann and Isolde Moser - of publishing their sister's 'War Diary' naturally we seized it. The meeting that hurried text describes - between a young woman beginning to be a writer and a young man who could talk to her about writers - will stand as an emblem of friendship and free exchange across the frontiers, after the most determined effort in human history to prevent such friendships and such exchanges for ever.

We should like to thank readers of *MPT* for putting up with any subscription or distribution problems they may have experienced over the past few months during the transferral of the administration of the magazine to Oxford. You may like to know that we have now been lucky enough, thanks to the generosity of the Arts Council, to appoint the excellent Deborah de Kock as our new Administrator. This will certainly mean that we shall be able to run the magazine more efficiently. Deborah will be dealing with the business side of *MPT*, and may be contacted at administrator@mptmagazine.com

May we also remind you that you can now subscribe online: www.mptmagazine.com.
Details of subscription rates appear on page 152

David and Helen Constantine
May 2005

Akhmatova on the South Bank

Ruth Borthwick

Anna of all the Russias: Translating Akhmatova

POETRY International, the South Bank Centre's biennial festival cele-
brating poetry from round the world, has always had an eye eastwards,
looking to Russia. Partly this lies in the origins of the festival at the height
of the Cold War, when Ted Hughes and Patrick Garland determined to
bring dissident voices from the Soviet empire to a western audience.
Mostly it is because of the extraordinary poetry written by Russians, past
and present.

The opening night of Poetry International features new poems written
by leading contemporary poets in honour of a great poet whose legacy
still inspires us today. For previous festivals we chose poets such as Dante
and Lorca, and the idea to have Anna Akhmatova as our subject came
from a conversation with Elaine Feinstein, who was steeped in research
for a forthcoming biography.

Anna Akhmatova began writing at a time when 'to think of a woman as
a poet was absurd', as she once remarked ironically. Her genius soared
above any such category, yet the human price she had to pay for that tri-
umph was as a wife and mother. She became the voice of a whole peo-
ple's suffering under Stalinist oppression, and it might have been expect-
ed that with the collapse of Communism she would have lost her iconic
stature. Instead, her poems are loved across the world.

As we looked at the poems, it was clear that the great themes of love,
freedom and patriotism were eternally significant and that Akhmatova's
style raised issues about the use of language in a restricted society. Elaine
and I came up with a list of poets whom we would invite to engage with
the project, and we were off. Elaine acted as Editor, discussing the choic-
es of poems with the writers and the poet; and translator Sasha Dugdale
eagerly accepted the challenge of writing her own poems, as well as pro-
ducing literals for the non-Russian speakers. Our poets also included
Colette Bryce, Poetry International's Poet in Residence; Michael
Donaghy; Carol Ann Duffy; Marilyn Hacker; Jo Shapcott and George
Szirtes. Elaine, too, wrote new poems and an introduction that she read
on the night.

The poets signed up in February 2004, worked on the poems through-
out the spring and on Saturday 23 October they took to the stage in the
Purcell Room. Sadly Michael Donaghy was not among them. After sub-
mitting his poems, he went to teach in Spain at the end of the summer

and on his return died of a brain haemorrhage, suddenly. We, along with all those who loved Michael and his poetry, mourned him. On the night, his glorious poems were read by Carol Ann. She was joined on stage by all the poets who had been part of the project and we paid our respects.

Akhmatova's poems also stimulated new work by young people at Poetry International, who, as members of Furnace, worked with Colette Bryce in workshops over three days at the Royal Festival Hall to produce a booklet of poems entitled *Freedom*. Furnace was set up as a collaborative project between two agencies, Apples & Snakes and Spread the Word, to develop young people in their writing and performance skills. As Colette herself commented: 'What would a group of young, hip, performance poets in twenty-first century London have in common with the great, austere Russian poet? Quite a lot it seems.' The resulting poems demonstrate how language acquires new meanings across the centuries, and still resonates for a young generation of poets on the threshold of their lives. I'd like to think that Anna Akhmatova would have been thrilled to know that her poetry lives on in this way and that she still inspires us.

Elaine Feinstein An Evening for Akhmatova

IT IS is now almost two years since Ruth Borthwick and I first discussed an evening at the Purcell room in honour of Anna Akhmatova. The plan was to involve several contemporary English poets who would translate her work into their own voice. I was delighted. I've been in love with Russian poetry ever since I first began to translate Marina Tsvetaeva in 1969, and have always believed that the best versions of Russian poems are made by practising poets in collaboration with a linguist who can offer literal versions.

I was working at the time on a biography of Akhmatova, out this June from Weidenfeld and Nicholson, and was preoccupied by her courage and dignity. It was not an easy task. In Tsvetaeva, I had been able to recognise myself, at least in her impracticality and eccentricity; Akhmatova was a very different creature: a great beauty, loved by many men. Her poetry had a classical restraint, while Tsvetaeva liked to express her emotions nakedly, and felt a constant pressure to invent new forms.

Akhmatova writes barely and lucidly, using little imagery, and relying on a colloquial music. This simplicity is not easy to transform into English poetry, but she has already attracted many fine translators, perhaps because the story of her stoical endurance under Stalin made her an inspiration for millions. In my biography, I translated all her poems afresh as this was the best way I knew to enter her inner world.

Sasha Dugdale, one of the poets invited to take part in the Purcell reading, is a Russian speaker, and she was able to supply literal versions of the poems I had chosen to Colette Bryce, Michael Donaghy, Carol Ann Duffy, Marilyn Hacker, Jo Shapcott and George Szirtes. I distributed the poems according to my own sense of the poets involved. For instance, several of the poems I asked George Szirtes to translate dealt with exile; and I looked out quirky, ironic poems for Carol Ann Duffy. Both Marilyn Hacker and Michael Donaghy wanted to write poems which arose from their reading of Akhmatova, rather than translating particular poems. It is one of my most painful memories that Michael Donaghy, whom I knew as a friend as well as admiring his poetry, died a few days before the Purcell reading.

There were occasional problems . I loved Carol Ann's 'The Toast', but in the last line of her version she suggests Akhmatova had no belief in the existence of God. Akhmatova's poem makes a different point: God does not intervene to save anyone. I imagined the auditorium filled with people who knew the original poem, and begged her to clarify the change of meaning . She made no objection.

The six poems I picked for myself span Akhmatova's whole life. Here are four of them. One of the few which can with any confidence be attributed to her relationship with her first husband, Nikolai Gumilyov was written in 1910.

He loved three things in this world:
White peacocks, evensong
And faded maps of America.
He hated it when children cried.
He hated tea with raspberry jam, and
Any female hysteria in his life.
Now imagine it: I was his wife.

Another poem, dated January 1914, is clearly directed at one of her lovers.

Everything was the same. A fine
Snowstorm blew at the windows.
Even I had not changed very much -
Until that man approached me.

'What do you want?' I asked him.
'To be with you in Hell,' he replied.
I laughed at that: 'You prophesy
Disaster for both of us.'

Then raising his dry hand
He lightly brushed the flowers:
'Tell me, how do men kiss you?
Tell me how you kiss.'

Then he stared at my rings
With fixed and weary eyes
And not one muscle moved
In his vicious, radiant face.

I know what comforts him.
He understands precisely:
That he needs nothing from me
While I can refuse him nothing.

During the Second World War Akhmataova was evacuated to Tashkent, and there suffered from typhus. In a strange poem, written much later and marked 'in a high fever', her thoughts seem to be wandering among old friends. The lyric is preceded by epigraphs from Pasternak and Mandelstam, and as she broods over her fellow poets, she calls up Marina Tsvetaeva who committed suicide in Yelabuga during the War.

Herewith I now renounce all earthly goods,
Whatever worldly property I own,
The spirit that is guardian of this place is
Only an old tree stump standing in water.
We are no more than guests upon this earth,
To live, essentially, no more than habit ...
I overhear two friendly voices now,
Speaking to one another in the air.

Did I say two? ... Look, by the eastern wall
Where raspberry canes are tangling with each other
There is a fresh, dark elderberry branch -
And that is like a letter from Marina.

I also read a section from *Requiem*, Akhmatova's great poem which describes waiting in line outside the Kresty prison. She began writing it in 1940 when her son Lev was held in the Gulag, and she knew she was under constant supervision. Each lyric from that sequence had to be committed to memory, and burned in an ash tray as soon as it was complete. What follows is part of the Epilogue.

Epilogue

If this country ever should decide
To dedicate a monument to me

I would accept that honour only
On condition the memorial stands

Not by the sea where I was born -
All my ties with the sea are broken -

Nor by the pine stump in the Tsar's garden
Where a sad ghost still looks for me

But here, where I stood for three hundred hours
Outside these gates that never opened once,

In case in blissful death I might perhaps
Forget the rumbling of those Black Marias

Or how the hated door banged shut against
An old woman howling like an animal.

Then let the melting flakes flow down
Over bronze eyelids as if they were tears,

And may a prison dove coo in the distance
While the ships on the Neva sail quietly on.

Colette Bryce Six Poems

MAKING successful versions of poems seems to me to depend upon achieving the tension and the music anew, as these are the untranslatable elements. Attempting to solve the puzzle that is the translated poem is similar to how I approach my own work, when I have a first draft safely captured. With these poems of Anna Akhmatova, I received basic literals and was more concerned with being true to the essence of the poem than in creating a strict word-for-word translation. That said, I have remained quite faithful to the originals, and have attempted to convey the poet's voice in English.

I related to these poems, and this allowed me to inhabit them during the writing process. I include here some brief notes on context, which may be of interest to readers, as they were to me while making these versions.

'Under a dark veil', and 'He was young, anxious, jealous' are early poems, both referring, most probably, to the poet's unhappy marriage to Nikolai Gumilyov and their wretchedness together.

'I hid my heart from you' was written near the end of Akhmatova's fifteen-year relationship with the art historian Nikolai Punin, during which she shared the Punin apartment with his wife and daughter. 'Splitting Up' also refers to this relationship. The couple finally separated in 1938. Their time together coincided with the poet's least productive period; she claimed not to have written a poem for thirteen years.

'Dante' is a personal favourite. The quote from the *Inferno*, 'Il mio bel San Giovanni', leads on to a reference to the baptistery of the Cathedral in Florence, 'the fair sheepfold where I slept as a lamb'. Dante was banished from the city for his political beliefs in 1302. Over a decade later he was offered a deal to return on the condition that he would perform a humiliating public repentance, which he rejected. The poem is believed to be a coded reference to her friend the poet Osip Mandelstam, who was in exile in Voronezh at the time, and who later died in exile.

The last poem is dedicated to a local child, Valya Smirnov, whom the poet befriended while living in Fountain House in the 1930s. The boy perished during the Siege of Leningrad, after Akhmatova was removed to Tashkent. In a small companion piece she wrote 'Through the bombardment is heard / The voice of a child'.

Under a dark veil she wrung her hands...

Under a dark veil she wrung her hands...
'What makes you grieve like this?'
I have made my lover drunk
with a bitter sadness.

I'll never forget it. He left, reeling,
his mouth twisted, desolate...
I ran downstairs, ran into the courtyard,
managed to catch him opening the gate

and begged him: 'It was all a joke, don't leave,
please... I will lose my mind!'
But he only smiled, calmly, terribly,
and said to me: 'Get inside out of the wind.'

1911

He was young, anxious, jealous...

He was young, anxious, jealous.
His love was like the heat of the sun
but he killed my white bird
as he could not bear her singing of the past.

Sunset. Into the room he strides:
'Love, laugh, write poetry!' he orders me.
I buried the bird
by the well, near the alder tree.

I promised him I wouldn't cry
but my heart set to a stone,
and now it seems that everywhere
I turn, I hear her sweet song.

1914

I hid my heart from you...

I hid my heart from you
as if I had gone and drowned it in the Neva.
Now, tamed, my wings clipped,
I live here in your home.
Only... at night, strange sounds.
What can they be, under the darkness?
Lindens in the Palace gardens...
The hushed notes of the house ghosts...

The soft black whisper of disaster,
cautiously, like rising water,
draws close to my ear
and murmurs - it is a messenger -
You wanted comfort,
now where is your comfort?

1936

Splitting Up

Not weeks, not months - years
of splitting up. Here's
to raw freedom,
to the first grey hairs!

No more lies. No more betrayals.
And no more listening, late into the night,
to the overwhelming evidence
that I was always right.

1940

Dante

'Il mio bel San Giovanni…'

Even after his death he did not return
to the fold of his native Florence.
This song is in praise of one
who left without a backward glance.
Nightfall: flames, a last embrace;
outside, the siren wail of fate.
Even in hell he cursed her,
and in paradise, could not forget her,
but neither would he stoop to walk,
in a hair shirt, with lighted candle,
barefoot, her beloved streets,
base, perfidious, yearned for…

1936

Knock with your little fist, child…
(In memory of a Leningrad boy, my neighbour, Valya Smirnov)

Knock with your little fist, child,
I will open, as I always did.
I live beyond the mountain now,
beyond the desert, the wind and the heat,
but I will never forget you.
I didn't hear you cry.
I didn't hear you beg for food.

Bring me a sprig from the maple tree,
or just a simple handful of grass,
the way you did last spring.
Bring me, cupped in your small hands,
some clear, pure water from our Neva
and I will rinse the blood
from your golden hair.

1942

Sasha Dugdale Five Poems

AKHMATOVA'S poetry has always entranced me. Mostly for its sonorous, lyrical qualities. When I was a student, I learnt some of *Requiem* and the shorter lyrics off by heart and I used to recite them to myself. Many of my Russian women friends admit to having been Akhmatova groupies in their teens and I notice rather cynically now that she fills the Plath-gap in Russia. I learnt her words unquestioningly and chanted them, so when I went back to translate them it rather confounded me to discover that I didn't like her very much. I didn't like her emotional dependency, her masochism, the rather hysterical voice of her love poems. However I did like the sound of them and the shape of them, and that is just what I felt would be lost in translation. I was anxious that her love songs in my translations would become unleavened free verse, or, worse still, strained rhyme, and that the emotional load would seem ridiculous and old-fashioned without the formal control of the original.

In the process of translating I discovered that the sentiments weren't as alien to me as I had thought. Really, all Akhmatova did was extract every last drop of narrative from the situations she found herself in or could imagine herself in. It is heady stuff, when distilled, but my mistake was to imagine on some level that *she lived like that* or that *the reader should live like that.* The worst mistake a reader can make. The narratives of Akhmatova's poetry are as artificial and contrived as the forms, and that at least becomes clear in translation. But she sets an example in living life in such a hungry way and harvesting so much from it.

I resolved to make my translations as worked-over as the originals and to try to give some sense of the desperate hunger for life and experience which I found in them. I followed most of the formal structures, not all, and translated rather than adapted - except in the poem 'The purple marks he left…' In this poem the lyrical voice describes the detail of the landscape, 'the real world', because she wants it all back after her blinding love affair. I felt the essence of the poem would not be altered if this detail was different, and so I located the poem in the vivid coastal landscape of the Shetlands where I was staying when I was working on it.

The immortelle is paper pink,
Clouds are stuck in a blue scrapbook,
The leaves are still bare and pale
On the park's single oak.

It's twilight here till gone twelve.
How good it is, so secluded and small.
On the gentlest matters, the endless miracles
The Lord's birds talk.

I am happy. Yet best of all
For me is a sloping forest path,
A simple bridge, a crooked one
And that my wait is almost done.

After Akhmatova

The purple marks he left
Have faded from my mind, the visions
In my head. There is a sea mist
Today, and the shadows of birds
On the water.

I can hear the shrill gannets
From the stacks, their ancient shapes
Hidden in the fog. The fulmars
Stand in the air close to us and call.

I was picking faded flowers on the cliffs -
Seapink and tiny spring squill.
Just now two puffins landed on the grass
With fish-filled beaks, and scuttled past.

I want it back, the real world,
To touch and grasp, blinded as I am -
Still I am healed, I have been cured
With departed love's icy calm.

Listen - I didn't sod off with the rest
When the enemy came calling. I
Stuck around. So now their sweet words
Of praise stick like fishbones in my gullet.
And I say:
Don't lay a finger on my music.

Still,

The ones forced to leave, to wander,
My heart contracts for them -
Without this country they are
Nothing
Sick,
Dimly lit prisoners
Crouching to gather foreign crumbs
Bitter solace.

You should

Know that back here we were burning
In the hottest part of the flame.
Our youth's remains charring, vanishing
Because we faced it out.
Every last blow.
I never once
Raised an arm
To protect myself.

One day.

One day they'll count it up,
Find every last hour
Worth it.
Still, for now, there is no one
Anywhere
Prouder
Simpler
With fewer tears
Than us.

Everything - taken, betrayed, traded,
Death's crow's-wing has flashed through the sky
We are skin and bones with the hunger of yearning -
Then suddenly, suddenly this light.

Day breathes cherry blossom through the leaves
Of a magical forest beyond city walls
The furthest corners of sheer July nights
Are reached for and touched by new stars.

And the miracle passes within a hair's breadth
Of our crumbling, blackened homes
None of us, none of us see it
But we've longed for it all of our lives.

I remember your words
As if from the edge of a cloud,

And with my words your nights
Became as bright as days.

We were torn from the earth
And soared as high as stars

Beyond despair and shame,
What is, what will be and was,

But as you live and wake
You hear me calling out.

And the door you left ajar
I don't have the strength to close.

Jo Shapcott Five Poems

IT IS hard for me to call these poems translations for the simple reason that I don't know Russian. I was given excellent literal translations by Alexandra Dugdale to work from and, in addition, I asked a Russian-speaking friend to read the poems to me in Russian to get a sense of the rhythm and the music. For all that, I still don't believe they are translations. Looking through them again, it's embarrassingly clear to me that I've unconsciously added to Akhmatova's poems more physicality, more sense of the body, which, I suppose, is integral to the way I think and write. This is clearest in the poem, 'We'll never drink . . .' where my lovers actually drink and breathe each other. Her lovers are more delicate, subtle. The poem 'The Cellar' is one that I chose because it seemed to me to represent an astonishing account of a descent into the unconscious which eventually becomes quite frightening as the mind becomes detached from its normal daylight ways of looking and thinking. I liked very much the way she spoke, in her poems, to her readers and even to her poems, calling the last poem she'd written just a 'hungry little thing'. Poems and readers are as real and important as lovers, friends, family. In 'The Reader', I loved the way she imagined her own readers as treasures, as reproachers, and her poems, in some way, a confession to them. If anything, my ending is even more questioning than hers: are the readers 'still here, still here?' I was given one of her most famous poems, 'Wild honey' to work on. I stayed as close as possible to the tight, beautiful images she creates for the first section of the poem. In the second half, she uses the figure of Pontius Pilate, washing his hands in front of the people. I changed him to George Bush, reasoning (rightly or wrongly, I don't know) that she might have spoken more frankly, if she could; and since I live in a more open time and place, then I should.

We'll never drink each other again
from the same glass, drink water or wine,
we'll never kiss in the early morning,
nor look into each other through the same night window.
You breathe in the sun, me the moon,
but breathing each other keeps us alive.

I walk around inhaling your tenderness,
and you've pocketed my smile for company,
but I know I've kissed fear into your grey eyes
because you've stroked pain into mine.
We can't meet often, can't meet for long.
There's a kind of peace in it.

At least your voice is the honey in my poems,
and in your poems my breath hums.
If we made a bonfire of all the pages
it might scorch oblivion or our fear . . .
and you would know how very dear you are,
you, your dry open mouth, how dear.

The Cellar

Don't think that I live grieving
or that the past eats me up.
I don't often visit memory
but it always makes a fool of me.
When I take my torch down into the cellar
an avalanche crashes behind me,
tumbles down the narrow staircase.
The torch dazzles and dies, I can't go back,
It's onwards into enemy territory.
And I beg for mercy . . . But the cellar
stays dark and quiet. The holiday's over.
Good night ladies; good night, sweet ladies; good night . . .
my brain's died of this musty dark old age.
I'm too late, too bad for the light,
I can't show my face anywhere
but my fingertips make pictures on the walls
and I'm warmed by what I touch. Wonderful.
Through mould, fume and dust
the sparkle of two emeralds says
it's the cat's miaow and so am I. Home.

But which way's home and where's my mind?

*

Now no one will listen to poems.
The prophesied days are here.
Listen, my last poem, the world's not a miracle
so stop tearing my heart, singing at me.

Not long ago you were free as a swallow,
following the arc of your morning flight,
but now you're just a hungry little thing
knocking unheard at strangers' doors.

The Reader

Poets, don't be too unhappy
and don't be secretive. Oh no!
Fling yourself open wide
so that everyone can see through you.

And footlights are a hazard,
making everything dead and bright,
and the cold halo of the spotlight
will mark your brow.

Every reader is a secret,
like treasure in the ground,
even the most recent odd one,
emerging from the silence.

They are everything, these readers,
hidden from us by the nature
of what we do, perhaps crying
helplessly somewhere, sometime,

stuck in too much twilight,
and shadow, and too much cold,
all those unfamiliar eyes
talking to me until dawn.

They reproach me over some things
and agree with me over others,
it's a strange, silent confession
I want to mistake for conversation.

The century's nearly gone
and I'm in a tight place
but the readers are still here,
still here, still here, still here?

Wild honey smells like freedom,
dust - like a ray of sun.
violets - like a girl's mouth,
and gold smells like nothing.
Honeysuckle smells like water,
and an apple - like love.
But finally we've understood
that blood smells just like blood.

And in vain the president from Texas
washed his hands in front of the people,
while cameras flashed and correspondents shouted;
and the British minister tried to scrub
the red splashes from his narrow palms
in the basement bathroom, outside
the strangers bar, in the Palace of Westminster.

George Szirtes (with Veronika Krasnova) Six Poems

MY WORK in translation has mostly been from Hungarian, that being chronologically my first language. I began in 1984 with poetry, verse plays and went on to fiction, while continuing to translate poetry, so the habit of translation is deeply ingrained in me by now. I expect to translate: I enjoy translating. When I first began I had help, much as almost all writer-translators from Hungarian did, from Hungarian writers, but gradually, as I recovered my half-forgotten first language, I began to work on my own, relying on editors to correct me.

I don't speak Russian but knew the work of Anna Akhmatova in various translations, chiefly Richard McKane's and was, in this case, given precisely the kind of help the Hungarians used to give me by the excellent Sasha Dugdale. Luckily for me, I also had a Russian friend Veronika Krasnova down the road who was working on her PhD on Russian poetry in translation. I had done a little Mandelstam for her as an experiment, and her views and readings were invaluable to me, which is why I would like her name to stand by mine as translator.

The first and most difficult task of a translator is, as I see it, to understand the poem. I don't mean the words, but somehow to see the ghost in the machine, to see what it is that gives that particular form of words life. Without this nothing can be done. I am aware that this sounds far too simple, because the process of reading is also the process of translation, so the life in the original begins to kindle, then overlap with, the life of the developing translation. The translator, if a poet, seeks that life and is used to seeing it develop in his or her own work. Nor is that 'life', if I may give the word its proper inverted commas at this stage, independent of all the elements that seem to comprise it. There is compromise and conversation throughout.

And there are risks to be taken. The biggest risk I took was in 'There is a secret line...' where the excitement seemed to lie not just in the metaphorical hand touching the metaphorical heart but in the implication of a real hand on a real breast. I think, feel, am certain, that the sense is there in the original, that there should be a sharp intake of breath at that point. The life is there. The other issue is that of form which is too complex for a short note like this. To put it simply I don't believe that form is decoration. I believe that, once employed, it is structural in the development of the poem and is an essential part of the voice. Not that forms replicate each other in different languages: they seek echoes, no more. But I have tried to provide such echoes.

Lot's Wife
(Genesis)

And the righteous man followed the vast blinding figure
Of the angel. Across black mountains lay their track.
But the voice of anxiety was shrill in his wife's ear:
It's not too late yet, there's time to look back

At the rose-red towers of the city, your Sodom,
At familiar courtyards where you would sing and spin,
At the deserted windows of the house where you lived
With the good man, your husband, and the children you bore him.

And so she glanced back and the pain at once bound her,
Her eyes were blind, however she made them round;
Her body grew transparent, turned to a pillar of salt,
Her once quick feet were fast rooted to the ground.

Who is there now to mourn for this woman?
Was she not least of those who perished that day?
My heart alone will not let me forget her
Who for a single glance gave her one life away.

1922-24

Seven hundred years I've been away…

Seven hundred years I've been away
But nothing's changed here, so to speak,
The same ineffable grace pouring
From the same impregnable peak

Same choirs of stars and waters
Same constellations, same black sky
Same seed in the same wind
Same mothers singing the same lullaby

My ancestral house stands firm
On Asian soil, why fret about it.
I'll be back soon enough. Let hedges bloom,
Let fountains gush pure water. Let them spout it.

Tashkent 1944

Despite all your promises...

Despite all your promises
You ran off with my ring
And abandoned me in the depths,
Helpless, without a thing..

So why last night's spectral visitation?
Why send him to me?
Young he was, cute, red-headed and lean
Wholly feminine,
Wailing like a hired mourner
And whispering insidiously
Of Rome, of Paris, and how
He really cannot do without me now.

Never mind shame, never mind the clink,

I'll manage without him fine, I think.

1961

There is a secret line...

There is a secret line between people who are close
Beyond which doting or desire may not tread,
However the heart shatters or explodes,
However the lips fuse in silent dread.

Friendship too is useless, however fierce
Or fiery the joy of it was long ago
When nothing bound the spirit to the body's affairs
With that langorous afterglow.

It's madness to approach that line, and the agony
Of touching it is more than we can bear,
So you will understand why my heart suddenly
Stops beating when you put your hand on it, right there.

1915

We thought that we were beggars...

We thought that we were beggars and had nothing
But as, one by one, we lost possessions and everyday
Became a ritual catalogue of loss,
We started writing songs about
The remarkable generosity
Of God, and how wealthy we had been
In the days of our beggary.

1915

Dante
Il mio San Giovanni...

Even after his death he kept well clear
Of the ancient Florence of his exiling.
It is for the man who did not reappear
Or once look back that now this song I sing.
Torchlight, darkness, a last embrace, then gone,
Past city limits to grim squawks of fate.
From hell he saw her and piled curses on,
But still recalled her, once through heaven's gate,
Where barefoot, hair-shirted and lovesick,
He did not walk the perfidious and low
Streets of Florence carrying a candlestick,
Pining for the city where he could not go.

1936

Marilyn Hacker 'For Anna Akhmatova'

THIS poem is neither a translation nor an 'imitation' of Akhmatova, but a poem in reponse to this immense poet/recognizable woman, and her themes which continue to resonate in a contemporary world infected by war and silencings. I can't, alas, read Russian; as I AM a translator, from French, the idea of constructing poems from literal translations of world-renowned (and frequently translated) texts, while incapable myself of hearing or perceiving the nuances in language, form and sonority involved, the echoes and the connotations behind the lines, did not seem to me to be translation as I understand it. Having heard the resonant and pertinent versions produced for Poetry International by the other poet participants, I realise I was perhaps simply not equal to the task.

For Anna Akhmatova

Who had been in love with her that summer ? Did it matter ?
The incidental willow is what she would remember,
bare like a silver brooch on a sky of foxfur
during the winters of famine and deportations.
She wished she had something more cheerful to show them:
a list of the flowering shrubs in a city park,
lovers and toddlers asprawl behind rosebushes;
workers with mallets indulging in horseplay
while knocking partitions of sheetrock to splinters:
energy's avatars, feminine, masculine.
Forehead against the cold pane, she would always be
ten-and-a-half years older than the century.

*

She remembered Mother reading them Nekrasov
as they ate sardines with white cheese and tomatoes
while sun set late on the same seacoast where Tomis
had sheltered and repelled an exiled poet.
She would eat the same briny cheese in the heat of Tashkent
waiting for news from re-named Leningrad.

*

It had pleasured her, a language which incised
choreographed chance encounters, almost-uttered
words, eye-contact, electricity
of an evaded touch: she wrote about
brief summers, solitude's inebriation
in the dusk that fell at almost midnight.
(Louise Labé in a less clement climate,
with electricity and indoor plumbing.)
She and her friends and lovers chiselled lyrics
until the decade (what did they think of revolution?)
caught up with them, the elegant companions,
and set them to a different exercise.

*

(Which travelling companions would you pick?
Who would have chosen to endure Céline?
Pasternak wrote a paean to Stalin;
Donne, for Pascal, would be a heretic.)

*

Something held her back from choosing exile
when the exacting enterprise went rotten.
Russia was not her motherland: it was St Petersburg,
the birch-lined corridors of Tsarskoye Selo -
but she was not retained by bark-scales spreading
up her limbs, with a god's breath in her ears: there
were her threatened friends, her son in prison
(who would not understand her coded letters
or what had held her back from choosing exile
after she did the paperwork to place him
in the Russian Gymnasium in Paris
the year his father met a firing squad;
and Marina - who would not live long -
wrote, she would meet them at the train station).
Tinned fish, gas rings, staggering armchairs, stained toilets
- mass graves of compromising manuscripts.
Was her exigent Muse the despised dictator
who censored, exiled, starved, imprisoned, murdered,
hurting the prodigy of birch and willow
into her late genius of *débridement*?
'Submissive to you ? You must be out of your mind...'

*

How could she imagine, the 'gay little sinner', up
daybreak to dawn, the exactions of history ?
City rerouted for transit to labour camps,
first husband shot in prison, their son in prison,

then in a labour camp, on the front, then still in prison.
She, over fifty, grown aquiline, vigilant,
larger than life, 'casta diva', her arias
camouflaged witness, evoking the dailiness
veiled in translation or foreign geographies.
Can you, yourself, in your eyrie, imagine it
while an empire's gearshifts creak behind you?

*

She made her despair the Virgin's or Cleopatra's
- under the circumstances, not outrageous.
She would write in praise of peace brought by the tyrant
if her lines might evoke an adjective passed down
from underling to underling until
some hungry guard unlocked a door... It didn't
happen. Her son called her superficial.
Larger than life, with all her flaws apparent
she rolled on the floor and howled in indignation,
more like the peasant she had come to resemble
than Anna Comnena or Cleopatra
or the ikon of words who was asked by other women
at the prison wall 'Can you describe this?'

*

Once, in a youthful funk, she had made a poem of
her son (then just four) at her churchyard graveside
unable to resurrect his flighty mother
except to the balance sheet of her defections.
She was alone, and he was alive, in prison.
The impatient butterfly of Tsarskoye Selo
a solid matron, stood below the frozen
walls, with her permitted package, like the others -
whether they had been doting or neglectful mothers.

John Greening
'Coming Soon. *Remastered from the Old Norse*'

COMING SOON was the final poem in a book-length sequence about Iceland, written in 2001 after I had been awarded a Society of Authors travel grant to visit Akureyri, my father's posting during the Second World War. As well as looking for Nissen huts and climbing lava flows, I found myself renewing an interest in Old Norse, which I had studied many years earlier. *Völuspá*, which had always intrigued me, is one of the most striking works to be found in the *Poetic Edda*, that collection of mythological verses which are 'to Iceland what the works of Hesiod and Homer are to Greece' (Paul B.Taylor). Although these poems were written down during the thirteenth century, their origins go back to an oral, musical tradition (fascinatingly recreated by the ensemble Sequentia on a recent CD). Usually translated as something like 'the prophecy of the wise woman' or 'the song of the sibyl', *Völuspá* is a vividly surreal account of the beginning and end of the world.

The idea of a 'seeress' revealing mysterious truths to the 'Allfather' Odin is difficult to convey in a modern translation, and I did not want to simply repeat what Auden had done in his lucid but luke-warm version (*Norse Poems*, 1981) or resort to the thundering biblical register of Henry Adams Bellows (*An Anthology of World Poetry*, ed Van Doren, 1929). I found that the imagery of apocalypse which pervades the poem, with its vision of 'Ragnarok', the 'doom of the gods', quickly metamorphosed into something cinematic, as if the only equivalent language was the hyperbole and trickery of the Hollywood trailer. *Völuspá's* slogan-like repetitions, exaggerations, use of improbable names, unexpected juxtapositions and gaudy gestures seemed ripe for such treatment. Besides, Hollywood's actors had for long enough been treated like gods and goddesses: here was a chance to turn the tables. 'Coming Soon' was intended, then, to be a somewhat playful version of the last two-thirds of the Icelandic original (skipping the creation myths), from the same postmodern stable as Baz Luhrmann's *Romeo+Juliet* - a 'remastering', an irreverently sardonic scenario for the end of the world.

Within days of finishing the translation, however, I found myself reading it in a very different way. I had barely printed it off and decided on the title, when 9/11 hit our television screens. Suddenly, the disaster movie imagery did not seem so ironic. My metamorphosis of the sibyl's prophecies into what had seemed a blockbuster fantasy now felt unnervingly like a news report. Something sulphurously modern bubbles in the depths of this extraordinary thousand-year-old poem.

Coming Soon
Remastered from the Old Norse

Alone in my humming suite, the ancient
impresario himself came gazing at me.
What are you after? What are you up to?
I know it all, Odin, even where your eye is.

Deep in Mimir's pool, his pool
of many screens, from which, from your blindness,
each morning he drinks your health, this Head
of Intelligence. Then what? Shall I go on?

All the hardware and software you offered me
as payment for my twenty-four hour news,
my propaganda and public service...
I see beyond this narrow orbit.

I see Valkyries auditioning on all sides
for their part in the great epic of the gods.
Skuld has a contract, so has Skögul.
Gunnur, Hildur, Göndul and Geirskögul -
these are the starlets who appear with Odin
on the wide silver world-screen, Valkyries.

The Fate of Baldr or *The Bleeding God*
are the working titles. This feature of Odin's
begins with a close-up of that spindly beauty,
full-grown, top billing, the mistletoe.

From that one opening shot was shaped
a blockbuster of a disaster movie
directed by Höður, though even as he did so
the sequel was entering post-production

(in which the newborn Odin android
vows he will track down Baldr's murderer
to the soundtrack of his mother weeping, weeping
for Valhalla.)
                    Then what? Shall I go on?

A long-shot of someone slumped in the badlands
(subtitle: *Cauldron*), a trouble-maker, looking
remarkably like... The camera pulls back
to show Loki and Loki's wife, not happy.
                    Then what? Shall I go on?

Dissolve: from the east through toxic valleys
Slith meanders between the arms dumps.
Slow pan across the northern landscape
of Niðavöllum Plain to a hall of gold
for the Sino hordes, then one - a brimming
beer-hall - for Brimir the Terrible.

Now cut to a bunker beyond the sun's reach,
on the shores of the dead. Its entrance looks north.
Radiation seeps through its airvent.
Its roof is a chain reaction of snakebones.

There in a montage are the thousand extras -
perjurers, murderers, seducers of wives.
The Daily Niðhogg guzzles on the corpses.
And the Nightly Wolf crunches their bones.

An old bitch sits in the east, in Ironwood,
where she's raised the litter of creatures from whom
will come the one who will tear down the moon,
the one who will home in on you like a warhead.

Already it gorges on internal organs,
spatters the heavens with plasma and lights.
The sun is black for summers unimaginable:
a nuclear winter.
                    Then what? Shall I go on?

Sitting in a bomb-shelter, twangling his banjo,
the giant's janitor, cheerful Eggþér.
Above him, from Mutant Wood, the crowing
of Fjalar, the red punk cockerel.

Higher than the gods, castrato Gullinkambi
arias armies awake in their barracks.
Another - skulking in the earth - croons
the colour of hopelessness from Hel's halls.

Garmr howls his feedback at the opening
to the final scene, in Gnipahelli - but he'll
be cut. The title will be *Ragnarok*.
The posters will slogan and blare its triumph:

Brother murders brother. Sister sister.
The world gone wild. A plague of promiscuity.
Gun-time. Bomb-time. There's nowhere to hide.
Wind-hour. Wolf-hour. The world spun mad.
Mercy? Mercy is only for innocents.

Children go on playing, but the clear
call of the siren has tripped the countdown.
Heimdall blasts heaven with megawatts.
Odin consults his Head of Intelligence.

The world-web shivers, the system
hacked and trembling, the lone anarchist
breaks loose and the viruses spread.
How are the fatcats? How are the mice?

The radio masts are trembling, the gods
are talking, trapped workmen wail
in the lift they repaired.
                        Then what? Shall I go on?

Garmr howls his feedback at the opening
to the final scene, in Gnipahelli - but he'll
be cut. The title will be *Ragnarok*.
The posters will slogan and blare its triumph.

Computer animation: Hrymur in his tank
against Jörmungandur. Sinuous snake-
battle, smashing backs of breakers.
Kamikaze eagle targeting corpses,
shrieking delight as Naglfar is freed.

Muspell's fleet sweeps from the east
Loki piloting marine commandos
from giantland, trailing giant hunger.

Surt whisks from the south, his chopper
chopping the treetops, his rotors
like beams from the sun of battlegods.
Peaks shudder. Camp-women scatter.
The dead throng the path from Hel
and heaven (this could be real) crumbles.

Hlin is hit by his worst luck
as Odin enters to fight with the wolf
and (split-screen) Freyr meets Surt.
Music: *A Lament for the Lost Friend.*

Garmr howls his feedback at the opening
to the final scene, in Gnipahelli - but he'll
be cut. The title will be *Ragnarok.*
The posters will slogan and blare its triumph.

And introducing Viðar (Odin dynasty)
who takes out Valdr in a brief scene's
vengeance for how his father has been treated:
with a single bullet.

The world-serpent is unravelling from its hard-drive
and rising up as high as heaven's gates.
It's time for Thor. He hammerblows
at the beast in fury, hacks his way into
this macrocircuited earth-locker.

The sun turns black. The land runs to sea.
The bright stars shrink from the sky.
Geysers cannon at fire's wild
pro-life demonstration, scorching the gods.

Garmr howls his feedback at the opening
to the final scene, in Gnipahelli - but he'll
be cut. The title will be *Ragnarok.*
The posters will slogan and blare its triumph.

Filter: the earth green once more,
rising for a second time from the ocean,
the waterfalls tumbling, an eagle crossing
the hills, hunting fish. (Strings)

The gods meet again at Iðavelli,
discuss the world situation and consider
the Great Thoughts and Teachings of Odin.

The film ends as we see in the long grass
the wonderful chess-pieces, carved of gold,
the ones they had used. Slow motion. Sepia.

Crops growing without being planted.
Wickedness vanishing. Baldr returning
to reenter with Hoðr and the others the gates
of Valhalla, the heavenly gods' home.
                    (Final leitmotif and credits)

                    Then what? Shall I go on?

In small frame, Hoenir takes out
(light relief) the divining rods
and the sons of Baldr and Hoðr are seen
relaxing in their ranch: *WINDY REALMS*...

                    Then what? Shall I go on?

Soft focus: a hall rising
brighter than the sun, gold roofed.
It's Gimle Home. There they'll be cared for
the rest of their lives, those who gave
their lives for us.
                    Fade.
                         Lights up.

Now the dragon comes, dark, glittering,
swooping low from the rear stalls
carrying as he flies towards the screen
the bodies of the dead. It is Niðhogg.

I must go down.

Neil Philip

'Twenty-one glosses on poems from *The Greek Anthology*'

THESE very free versions of poems from *The Greek Anthology* began as an excuse to avoid doing more serious work. In a spirit of playfulness I began recasting Greek lyrics into a world of one-bar electric fires, credit cards, and charity shops. The result was a curious hybrid of ancient and modern - the Attic and the attic - which made me laugh. And so I carried on until I had written around a hundred, from which these are selected.

I began in each case with the literal prose translations in the Loeb edition (I did study Ancient Greek at school, but what shaky grasp of it I acquired then has deserted me now) and then re-cast them in the spirit of a be-bop musician riffing on a standard melody. The resulting verses are therefore the opposite of respectful word-for-word translations. Some of them do remain fairly close to the source poems, but others veer so far away as to be practically new creations. So I call them 'glosses', hoping to convey the spirit in which my texts both attend to and diverge from the originals.

Anonymous

Poverty and love
are making my life a misery.
Poverty is bad enough - but love!
It's unendurable.

Antipater of Thessalonika

One folding note
will buy you
this Europa's charms.
She has clean sheets,
and a one-bar electric fire
to take the chill off the air.
And best of all,
there's no need to take the trouble
to turn into a bull.

Antipholos

When Tereina was just a child,
I said, 'This one will break a few hearts
when she grows up.'
Everyone laughed - me too -
but now it's all come true.
Just to look at her
burns me up,
and look at her
is all I can do.
When I beg her
to put me out of my misery,
all she says is,
'I'm a virgin.'
This will be the death of me.

Bassus

Turn into a shower of gold, a swan,
a bull, a bird? That's too hard.
I'll leave such fancy tricks to Zeus,
and woo Corinna with a credit card.

Lucilius

All this stuff you buy -
exfoliating scrub,
moisturiser,
foundation,
highlighter,
lippy,
eye-shadow,
eye-liner,
mascara,
coloured contacts,
wash-in hair dye-
wouldn't a new face
work out cheaper?

Marcus Argentarius

I lie back, drunk,
and watch the golden stars
swirl round in the sky.
Stunned into silence,
I strum on my guitar,
and think I see both how they move
and why.

*

You can't beat the classics
for reading on the beach.
This year, Hesiod
was always within reach.
But as all the girls
were easy lays,
I didn't get far
with *Works and Days*.

*

When young Alcippe took me to her room
she put her finger to her lips and ssshhhed.
'My mother mustn't hear.'
And so I tiptoed about the place,
barely daring to breathe until I'd done the deed.
And then I heard her mother call,
'I hope you've saved some for me!'

*

Your name means bee,
Melissa, and my heart
tells me that it's from a bee
you learned your part.
Your mouth drips honey
as you kiss and cling,
while your hand dips in my purse
ready to sting.

You can never be too thin,
they say, though in Dioclea's case,
I'm not so sure.
Still, she's very sweet.
So I'll lie on her flat chest
and count myself lucky there's
so little between
her heart and mine.

*

Can you believe it, moon?
Sweet-smelling Ariste has left me.
Droop down your golden horns,
and let the shining stars sink in the sea.
For six days I have tracked the bitch
without once catching her scent.
But have no doubt -
the silver-throated hounds of love
will smell her out.

*

You only put those fishnets on
to tease, Lysidice.
Oh, wiggle your bum as well, why don't you?
And the way your dress clings to your body...
why bother wearing anything at all?
If you think it's so funny,
the way my prick rises at the very sight of you,
I'll drape your knickers across it.
Now you see it,
now you don't.
You're not the only one who can dance
the dance of the seven veils.

When you were rich, Sosicrates,
you called it love,
what you got up to with Menophila.
Now you're poor,
love's not an option anymore.
'How do you want me?' she used to say,
and 'Give it to me, big boy.'
Now it's 'Do I know you?'
and 'Where did you say you live?'
Poverty's the hard way to find out,
nobody loves you when you're down and out.

Pallades

Life's just like
amateur dramatics.
Join in
and it can be a laugh.
but it's a fucking bore
to watch.

*

If you haven't anything nice to say,
Don't say anything at all.
That's my firm rule.
But luckily saying spiteful things
is nice - so that's OK.

Paulos Silentiarus

I watched them
sucking face
for an eternity -
as if they longed
to climb into each other's hearts.
They shucked off their clothes,
and put each other's on.
Him in her flirty dress,
her in his jeans and leather jacket.
And then they went back to it
as if they hadn't eaten for a week.
You couldn't have parted them
without assistance from the Fire Brigade.
You and I were like that
once.

Philodemos

They're killing me,
the pair of them,
Demo and Thermion.
Thermion's a tart -
she'll open her legs
for anyone.
Demo's a convent girl -
I can't ever
get her alone.
When I'm with Demo
I can't get Thermion
out of my head.
When I'm with Thermion
I wish it was Demo
in my bed.

Rufinus

Save water, Prodike-
bath with a friend!
We'll crown each other with foam,
and knock back some champagne.
We haven't all that long
before our wrinkles mean
we're past our shag-by date -
not just that the water is too hot.

*

Didn't I warn you, Prodike,
we would grow old?
Now come the wrinkles and the grey hairs,
the sagging body and the slack mouth.
Who fancies us now?
They can smell the death on us.

*

How proud and scornful you were, Melissa,
in your glory days - with your flashing eyes,
your swan's neck
and your ankle chains -
when everybody wanted you.
Where' s it all gone?
Now your hair is cut by the junior,
your clothes are from the charity shop,
your jewellery is in hock.
Serves you right,
you snotty cow.

*

I love every single thing about you,
except for your awful
taste in men.

Paul Howard Versions of four sonnets by Giuseppe Belli

THE Romanesque sonneteer, Giuseppe Gioachino Belli (1791-1863), wrote some 2,279 sonnets in the Romanesque dialect and was probably prompted to do so after meeting and reading the work of the Milanese dialect poet Carlo Porta. The beauty of Belli's sonnets is that he uses the classical sonnet setting, but sends them up by couching them in dialect. So in order to come anywhere close to appreciating Belli in English, this rebellion has to be seated within the traditional English framework: the Petrarchan scheme of the original has to be transposed to the Shakespearean. Moreover, to translate Belli's Romanesque into Standard English is, in my view at least, to miss the most essential ingredient of his rebellion against the aulic high style, and so I think his dialect has to be transported into an English dialect with similar characteristics. I believe the varied assonance of the Yorkshire dialect goes some way to creating an equivalent of the coarse, double consonants of Belli's Romanesco.

La Bbona Famijja

Mi' nonna a un'or de notte che vviè ttata
se leva da filà, ppovera vecchia,
attizza un carboncello, sciapparecchia,
e mmaggnamo du' fronne d'inzalata.

Quarche vvorta se fàmo una frittata,
che ssi la metti ar lume sce se specchia
come fussi a ttraverzo d'un'orecchia:
quattro nosce, e la scena è tterminata.

Poi ner mentre ch'io, tata e Ccrementina
seguitamo un par d'ora dde sgoccetto,
lei sparecchia e arissetta la cuscina.

E appena visto er fonno ar bucaletto,
'na pissciatina, 'na sarvereggina,
e, in zanta pasce, sce n'annàmo a lletto.

Roma, 28 dicembre 1831

The Good Life

Mi gram when late at neet comes home t'owd man
drops the clothes she's knittin' us, poor owd pet,
sets us table an' warms room best she can,
an' we eat a few spuds, what we can get.

Nah'n again we'll 'ave us an omèlet,
an' if tha wer to 'old it up to t' sun
just like an ear, light'd shine reight thru' it:
a few crusts to nibble on, supper's done.

Then me, wi' t'owd man an' mi sister Grace
a couple o' hours o' suppin' pass,
while gram cleans up an' puts things back in place,
til we can see to t' bottom of us glass.

Next a quick piss and an 'ail mary,
an' straight up to bed in peace an' plenty.

Oxford, June 2004

La Vita Dell'Omo

Nove mesi a la puzza: poi in fassciola
tra sbasciucchi, lattime e llagrimoni:
poi p' er laccio, in ner crino, e in vesticciola,
cor torcolo e l'imbraghe pe ccarzoni.

Poi comincia er tormento de la scola,
l'abbeccè, le frustate, li ggeloni,
la rosalía, la cacca a la ssediola,
e un po' de scarlattina e vvormijjoni.

Poi viè ll'arte, er diggiuno, la fatica,
la piggione, le carcere, er governo,
lo spedale, li debbiti, la fica,

er zol d'istate, la neve d'inverno...
E pper urtimo, Iddio sce benedica,
viè la Morte, e ffinissce co l'inferno.

Roma, 18 gennaio 1833

The Life O' Man

Nine month long in't'stink: then a babby born
smother'd in kisses, milksop an' tears:
then t'reins, t'walker, an't'babby-cluwes worn,
w"t'bonnet an't'breeaks up to't'ears.

Then next up t'sufferin' o' skooel comes,
t'ABC, t'slipperin', t'canin', t'chilblains,
t'German measles, t'sittin' on't'bog wi't'runs,
bit o' small-pox, few scarlet fever pains.

Then there's t'livin' to mek, t'graftin' in't'muck,
t'fastin', t'guverment, t'prison if no rent,
t'ospit'l an't'debt an' mebee t'odd fuck:
t'summer sun, t'winter wet, what t'season's sent...

An' in't'end, God bless us, if truth to tell,
there's nowt but Deeath, and eternal 'ell.

Hawthornden Castle, 30th March 2005

Er Giorno Der Giudizzio

Cuattro angioloni co le tromme in bocca
se metteranno uno pe ccantone
a ssonà: poi co ttanto de voscione
cominceranno a ddì: ffora a cchi ttoca.

Allora vierà ssù una filastrocca
de schertri da la terra a ppecorone,
pe rripijjà ffigura de perzone,
come purcini attorno de la bbiocca.

E sta bbiocca sarà ddio bbenedetto,
che ne farà du' parte, bbianca, e nnera:
una pe annà in cantina, una sur tetto.

All'urtimo usscirà 'na sonajjera
d'Angioli, e, ccome si ss'annassi a lletto,
smorzeranno li lumi, e bbona sera.

25 novembre 1831

The Day O' Judgement

Fower angels w"t'trumpits at their lip
'll start to play, one on ev'ry corner,
by christ they won't 'alf let 'em bloody rip:
then shahtin', 'll sey: 'who's next, let's 'av'yer.'

Then score on score o' sheepish skeletuns
'll rammle up from t'earth to't'final pen,
to get their 'uman faces back, themsuns!
like little chicks what crowd round t'muther 'en.

This 'en 'll be t'oly fatther imsel,
and 'e'll divide 'em up in two on't'oof:
some black an' some white, so's 'e can tell
who's off to't'cellar an' who's off to't'roof.

Last a drove o'r'Angels 'll turn out't'light,
an' like it wer bedtime, that's it, night night.

Hawthornden Castle, 31st March 2005

Er Povero Ladro

Nun ce vò mmica tanto, Monziggnore,
de stà llí a ssede a ssentenzià la ggente
e dde dí: *cquesto è rreo, quest'è innoscente.*
Er punto forte è de vedejje er core.

Sa cquanti rei de drento hanno ppiú onore
che cchi de fora nun ha fffatto ggnente?
Sa llei che cchi ffa er male e sse ne pente
è mmezz'angelo e mmezzo peccatore?

Io sò lladro, lo so e mme ne vergoggno:
però ll'obbrigo suo saría de vede
si ho rrubbato pe vvizzio o ppe bbisoggno.

S'avería da capí cquer che sse pena
da un pover'omo, in cammio de stà a ssede
sentenzianno la ggente a ppanza piena.

21 novembre 1833

The Poor Thief

Yer'onor it really dunt tek a lot
to sit there passin' sentences on folk
an sey: "e's guilty, an' 'e's clearly not.'
T'ard bit's what's in their 'eart, tha's got to poke.

'Stha knaw, them wot seem oft so innocent
lack t'honour o' them on't'prison dinner?
'Stha knaw, when tha does bad and then repent
'alf o' thee's angel, 'alf o' thee's sinner?

Ah'm a thief, Ah knaw so, Ah feel t'shame:
but as a judge tha duty in each deed
ought be 't see why Ah'm in't'robbin' game,
whether it's aht o' vice or aht o'need.

Tha should see that t'poor man's pains 'ave no lull
stead o' sittin' there wi tha belly full.

Hawthornden Castle, 4th April 2005

Terence Dooley
A version of Raymond Queneau's 'La Pendule'

Si tu t'imagines...

RAYMOND QUENEAU, born in 1903 in Le Havre, was perhaps the most linguistically playful and inventive of twentieth-century French writers, and the funniest. Most accessible through his novels, of which *Zazie dans le métro* is only the best known, *Un rude hiver* and *Pierrot mon ami* equally recommendable, Queneau could do anything as a poet, and often did, both in his forms and in his content. In his verse *Bildungsroman, Chêne et chien* (the 'delicate etymology' of his two names), he explains how he was transformed from hound to oak with the help of a psychiatrist from Passy, and also Rimbaud, who liberated his subconscious:

> Je vivrai donc puisque cet homme
> m'a rendu, dit-il, clairvoyant...

He used rhyme and metre to lead him where they would, and co-founded the movement *Pataphysics* to promote the anarchic dissociation of ideas. He wrote a million million sonnets, that is to say ten sonnets where each line may be combined with any 13 of the other 139 to produce this number of possibilities. He modulates between the phonetically-spelt demotic, nursery nonsense, the scatological, the chanson, the real and the unreal, into the highest lyric register, and is either the translator's despair or his/her Ultima Thule.

'La Pendule' ('Brother Blues') was originally written in Queneau's own literary mockney, but I've translated it into the black street voice now widely used by the young of all races. An accent or slang may not be directly conveyed from one language to another. Jokes are also harder to translate than poems. In fact a poorly translated poem is like a badly told joke. No one's going to laugh.

La Pendule

1

Je mballadais sulles boulevards
Lorsque jrencontre lami Bidard
Il avait lair si estomaqué
Que jlui ai dmandé dsesspliquer
                 Eh bien voilà me dit-il
Jviens davaler ma pendule
Alors jvais chez lchirurgien
Car jai une peupeur de chien
Que ça mtombe dans les vestibules

2

Un mois après jrvois mon copain
Il avait lair toutskia dplus rupin
Alors je suis été ltrouver
Et jelavons sommé dsesspliquer
            Eh bien voilà me dit-il
Jgagne ma vie avec ma pendule
Jai su lestomac un petit cadran
Je vends lheure à tous les passants
En attendant qjai lcadran sulles vestibules

3

A la fin ltype issuissida
Lossquil eut vu qpersonne lopéra
Et comme jarrivais juste sul chantier
Moi je lui ai demandé qui vienne sesspliquer
Eh bien voilà me dit-il
Jen avais assez davoir une pendule
Ça m'empêchait ddormir la nuit
Pour la remonter fallait mfaire un trou dans ldos
Jpréfère être pendu que pendule

4

Lossquil fut mort jvais à son enterrment
Cétait lmatin ça mennuyait bien
Mais lossqui fut dans le trou ah skon rigola
Quand au fond dla bière le septième coup dmidi tinta
Eh bien voilà voilà voilà
Il avait avalé une pendule
Ça narrive pas à tous les chrétiens
Même à ceux quont un estomm de chien
Et du coeur dans les vestibules

Brother blues

I

I drug me down the street
Who I meet
Old two-feet

Looks so green
I say: Man,
Where you been?

Says: I ate a clock
Goin to the doc
Doc I say him: Unlock

Me up. Stop that tick
I so fray
It blow me away

II

Few weeks gone
Who come along
I say: How you doin

Says: I got the time
They ax the time
They pay me, ain't no crime

I got belly time they buy
I say: Bro' you high
You gonna die.

III

Third time he done
Tore hisself open
This time he goin

Where he caint come back.
Say why I cry
Says: I don' wanna die

Tick-tock won' shuddup
Won' stop
Windin' me up

Drilled a hole
In my back to wind it
Putsa another hole

In front behind it
Caint take the tick-it
So I lick it.

He die soon

XII

He die. I go
Puts him in the hole
He too young
I caint stand it.

He down there
Ring out twelve
Stand it you own
God damn self.

Kathleen Jamie Hölderlin into Scots. Two poems

CONFESSION time: my copy of David Constantine's translations of Hölderlin bears the stamp of a noted literary institution, because... well, because I nicked it.

I'm a poor reader of poetry, I tend to respond to the 'hit' or 'aura' of a poem. The 'hit' from Hölderlin was high, intoxicating, anxious, open. (Later I learned that Rilke had called him 'exposed' - perfect.) I thought 'What is this strange, keening, poignant voice, what on earth is he saying?' Also, there were *things* I liked... mountains, rivers, ships, birds. I hid the book in my bag. And having shamelessly stolen it, I continued to read it on the train journey home, which journey took me through Scottish mountains, along rivers, past lochs with swans floating there, so Hölderlin's landscapes took on a Scottish flavour. It seemed I was reading what we'd now call an eco-poet. There's an anxious earth-love in Hölderlin, and I liked that.

Scots is the language of lowland Scotland, not to be confused with Highland Gaelic. Most lowland Scots have some of it, a good few words or phrases. At its full-blown best, as in Lorimer's translation of the New Testament, it is at once earthy, wry, passionate, and majestic. Its status is still peculiar. Those of us over a certain age remember being forbidden to use it in school, or even at home if our parents were concerned that we should 'do well for ourselves'. Its demise was constantly proclaimed, but now its promotion is official policy, apparently.

Translating obliges one to slow down and read very, very carefully - and I wanted to do that with Hölderlin. Translating allowed me the chance to 'inhabit' him, and try to fathom him out. (I should say I have no German, I rely on Michael Hamburger's and David Constantine's translations, and David very kindly provides me with literal versions.) Also I wanted to try to develop my Scots into a more tensile, robust and elegant medium. Robert Burns achieves a lovely intimate apostrophising in Scots - consider 'To a Mountain Daisy', Hölderlin has it too, but it's hard to carry off in English, so I thought it would go well into Scots. As well, I wanted the chance to risk bigger emotional and rhetorical gestures than are commonly allowed in English, which is a language easily embarrassed.

After all this I'm sorry to say I've only translated four small pieces of Hölderlin into Scots, and have yet to dare tackle his big hymns or odes. But I will do more. The project is beset with the usual worries which speakers of archaic or minority languages will recognise. Is it legitimate to use a word never actually heard spoken, but gleaned from an old dictionary? What's the point of the project at all, when only about fifty folk will be able to read it? But then again, almost all English-language poets alive now in Scotland also write in Scots. Why? Because we can, because it's beautiful.

An die Parzen

Nur Einen Sommer gönnt, ihr Gewaltigen!
Und einen Herbst zu reifem Gesange mir,
Daß williger mein Herz, vom süßen
Spiele gesättiget, dann mir sterbe.

Die Seele, der im Leben ihr göttlich Recht
Nicht ward, sie ruht auch drunten im Orkus nicht;
Doch ist mir einst das Heil'ge, das am
Herzen mir liegt, das Gedicht gelungen,

Willkommen dann, o Stille der Schattenwelt!
Zufrieden bin ich, wenn auch mein Saitenspiel
Mich nicht hinab geleitet; Einmal
Lebt ich, wie Götter, und mehr bedarfs nicht.

Tae the Fates

Grant me, Po'ers, jist ane simmer mair
an ane maumie autumn,
that ma hairt, ripe wi sweet sang
's no sae swier for tae dee. A saul

in life denied divine richt
wil waunner Orcis disjaiskit; but syne
ah win whit's halie an maist
dear tae ma art - ane perfit poem -

I'll welcome the cauld, the quate mirk!
For though I maun lee ma herp
an gang doon wantin sang, Ah'd hae lived,
aince, lik the gods and aince is eneuch.

Hälfte des Lebens

Mit gelben Birnen hänget
Und voll mit wilden Rosen
Das Land in den See,
Ihr holden Schwäne,
Und trunken von Küssen
Tunkt ihr das Haupt
Ins heilignüchterne Wasser.

Weh mir, wo nehm' ich, wenn
Es Winter is, die Blumen, und wo
Den Sonnenschein,
Und Schatten der Erde?
Die Mauern stehn
Sprachlos und kalt, im Winde
Klirren die Fahnen.

Hauf o Life

Bien wi yella pears, fu
o wild roses, the braes
fa intil the loch;
ye mensefu' swans,
drunk wi kisses
dook yir heids
i the douce, the hailie watter.

But whaur, when winter's wi us
will ah fin flo'ers;
whaur the shadda
an sunlicht o the yird?
Dumbfounert, the wa's staun;
the cauld blast
claitters the wethervanes.

Josephine Balmer
The Word for Sorrow : A work begins its progress

LIKE all potentially promising plans, *The Word for Sorrow* came about by chance. After working simultaneously on two classically-veined projects, a translation of Catullus' shorter poems and a poetry collection, *Chasing Catullus*, I had long been promising myself a break from the classical world. And yet increasingly I found myself eying up Ovid's much-neglected poems of exile, *Tristia* and *Epistulae ex Ponto*, the epistolary verse written after the poet's sudden and mysterious exile from Rome to the Black Sea in AD 8. For some time I had been struck by the depth of raw emotion it displayed, as if the mask of classical literary artifice had crumbled away to reveal the pain of the man beneath (although Ovid, the master of disguise, could always have been adopting another). And then fate intervened.

One rainy spring day I was working on an initial translation from *Tristia* using the Perseus site's on-line Latin dictionary, when an electrical storm required me to log off . Turning to an old dictionary, bought at a village fête as a school-student, I noticed by chance an inscription on its fly-leaf which I must have seen many times over the years and yet barely registered: a name in faded ink and a date, early in 1900. Back on-line a few days later, I ran a search on the name, almost on a whim. The results were impressive: First World War documents and diaries relating to 1/1st regiment of the Royal Gloucester Hussars, posted to Gallipoli in 1915, to the Hellespont, near Ovid's own place of exile and which, by coincidence, Ovid had just described crossing in the poem I was translating. Following link after link, more and more connections were revealed; old photos of the regiment lined up on Cheltenham Station just before leaving for the east, bringing parallels with Ovid's famous poem describing his last night before exile. The eye-witness accounts detailing the sickness, deprivations and dangers of the Gallipoli campaign in which 50,000 Allied troops and 85,000 Turkish soldiers died, reminiscent of Ovid's own powerful laments about his conditions of exile. And so *The Word for Sorrow* came about, versions of Ovid's verse alongside original poems exploring the history of the second-hand dictionary used to translate it.

But how were Ovid's poems to be approached and how were they to be transformed? From the start I knew I didn't want to create another 'straightforward translation' (Peter Green's excellent 1994 Penguin edition already filled that role with aplomb). I knew, too, that I couldn't possibly hope to cover all of Ovid's exile poetry (there are around 95 poems in all in nine books). Similarly, I would need to be selective about what I used from each poem, as many ran to more than a hundred lines. Here, I soon realised, narrative drive would be the key; the poems and renditions had to spark off each other, to hold the dramatic tension between the two as each story progressed. For this reason I've condensed here and there, for example, in 'Burning Books', from *Tristia* 1.1., where I've used only the first eighty-two lines. In particular, I've found myself omitting many of Ovid's incessant appeals for clemency to the emperor Augustus, perhaps rather craven, let alone cringing, for modern tastes. I am keen, however, to retain Ovid's flashes of wit which didn't appear to have deserted him in exile, despite his protestations. It is also important for the poems to flow into each other. For this reason I've often mixed up the line order of Ovid's verse as well as condensing. For example, 'All at Sea', from *Tristia* 1.2., starts at line 15 of the Latin in order to provide a natural continuation from the end of the preceding poem, 'Hail.'

Yet the guiding force here, as ever, is fidelity. I start by working in detail on the text, poring over commentaries and scholarly studies, weighing up the various theories and arguments, the prolonged discussions over every nuance of the Latin, to produce in the first instance faithful, literal translations. Only then can versions be shaped, like an abstract painter, perhaps, using figurative sketches and constructions as a basis for refining image into pure form or colour. For as well as tracking Ovid's journey via my versions, I'm also looking for Ovid to creep into my own poems so that the two will have a truly symbiotic relationship. And so 'Dancing in the Dark' takes its cue from a line in Peter Green's translation of *Ex Ponto* IV.2., while 'The Horses' uses images from *Tristia* I.4.

For what is becoming clear as the work takes shape, is that there is far more here than a simple Gallipoli/Tomis or text/dictionary equation; just as Ovid's often ironic poetic voice interposes itself into his narrative, so can my own, offering a third story of discovery, the detective story running like an undercurrent beneath.

And just as Ovid writes about far more than his exile - his vocation as a poet, for example, or the wider role of the artist in social and political life - so there are also wider issues for me, such as the role of translation or indeed classical literature in today's world. There are other narratives too; the private writings - diaries, letters, photographs, even poetry - of British soldiers on the eastern front, many of which mention my dictionary's owner, as well the testimony of his daughter with whom I've been in contact, all providing, like Ovid's verse, striking source material.

The challenge now, of course - the eternal prayer - is to be worthy of this material. As in *Chasing Catullus*, recontextualisation and juxtaposition will be central to the creative process, the dialogue between text and translator, writer and subject, between original and version, poetry and translation. Most important of all, though, are the links forged between ancient and modern, past and present, the invisible lines that connect us to often surprising points in history, finding common ground in unexpected places, celebrating the common humanity that binds us, whether we live at the beginning of the first, the twentieth or the twenty-first century AD.

The following extract comes from the opening of the sequence, as Ovid makes his journey east, remembering his last days in Rome. Meanwhile the dictionary's secrets begin to be uncovered.

i. Back in Rome

Go on without me, book, but with my blessing,
back to our home town, the exile trespassing
(for you're not forbidden, banned where I am barred
although plain, scuffed, as black as my mourner's heart)
but if your page is smeared, your words left undefined,
those blots are from tears and now the tears are mine.
Go on, retrace my paths, tread the streets for me,
between the lines, in the cracks, set my feet free.
And if, in the crowd, there's one, just one, who asks,
tell them: 'yes, through me he still lives, still breathes - just
but without the good health he enjoyed before.'
Then snap shut: remember, less is always more;
you see, in this no-man's land, the soul's slow death,
my books might be read but my sins stay scarlet.
But if they're quick to judge, here's your alibi:
poetry should be drawn down from clear cold skies
not scrawled under clouds in the eye of the storm;
poetry requires calm, quiet recollection,
should taste of the stars and yet smell of the lamp
not salt-soured seas, harsh winds, rust of wintry damp.
Poetry's writing without fear: words can't be coaxed
when the knife is always pricking at your throat.
Show pity, then, all critics, be indulgent;
that this verse exists should cause astonishment;
(put Homer in my place, give him these dangers
and watch his high art fade, great voice grow fainter).
Besides, if you scrutinise this title page
you'll find nothing Amoral. That price is paid.
I know there are Gods who can be merciful
still I dread the hand that brought me to my fall;
for I've felt the crack of skies, roar of thunder
so I fear the storm always at my shoulder.

(from Tristia I.1)

ii. Hail

A dismal spring, first of a new millennium
and thirteen days (so far) of relentless rain;
lines are down, Perseus can't save the day,
no help now from latinvocabdotcom,
no hope but to return to the old addiction.
Like a reformed junkie needing one last shot
I slide the book down softly from the shelf,
dustier now, with that tell-tale whiff of rot.
Sudden hail taps on the window pane -
impatient late collection, rattled box,
slap of spade on long-buried inscription -
and there, as if still fresh, on the front page,
dual initials, double-barrelled surname:
A.E. Lyneham-Forgrave , 7th April 1900
scrawled in schoolboy boredom, thunder-stiff,
blood brown ink, faint as an old man's vein:
the bruising flare of chained sheet lightning
that flashes, strikes, then moves on
                              leaving everything changed

iii. All at Sea

sparks glitter, cloud to cloud
              thunder cracks, Jove-loud
water bombards our ship's creaking hull,
relentless battering ram, siege-gun.
We're lifted up, up, to touch the stars,
plunged down, down, to Hell's black jaws,
pitched into abyss as each swell sinks
(spray stops my lips as I speak, write this).
Look around: sky and sea, sea and sky,
one flecked white, other furrowed grey;
gales rage between, god-forsaken, fierce,
uncertain which element to serve.
I don't fear death just the way it comes:
save me now and death would be welcome
for if sea should subside, storm be lulled
 - if I live on, I live in exile.
I don't care for power or riches,
don't plough oceans for jewels, fine silks.
I'm no student on the tourist trail:
Athens, Alex, diversions of the Nile.

So why - *why?* - wish for propitious winds;
in Sarmatia this trail must end.
I pray for safe landing, far from home,
sigh that this road to hell seems too slow,
strive for Tomis, last stop of the world,
the Black Sea, ice-hard, hail-stiff, snow-whirled;
plead for safe passage - to Tomis! -
in searching out the light
                  I'm staring at darkness
                      (from *Tristia I.2.*)

iv. Dancing in the Dark

Light shrinks into dank leylandii,
seeps down through thirsty grass:
dew settles on cowed verge,
tangle of laurel, euonymus:
hours now of hunting down words,
battered, bloodied, empty-handed,
confidence trickling away fast;
writing poems that no one reads
as Ovid (trans. Green) sighed
is like dancing in the dark,
the gesture no one sees you mime.
And tonight I'm stumbling after,
trying not to tread on toes (or feet)
trying - as ever - to keep up.

Time, maybe, to shut down, log off,
brew the tea, feed the circling dog
as a last gamble, chance Google
sends lines sliding back into place -
the first star cued above the Ghyll,
cloud-sketched moon on dusk-sharp sky,
Orion traced, tiptoeing into shape -
that unexpected hit of serendipity
reels down same name, new date,
a full-grown, fresh-joined regiment:
Royal Gloucester Hussars, 1915,
Palestine, Turkey, Gallipoli
(school Latin not required on trip)
another long exile in the east.

v. Last Night

So the hour had come. I could delay no further;
my bad-luck star had risen, hate-bright Lucifer
(how often had I rebuked those scurrying past:
'reflect where we are going, what we leave, don't rush.'
How many times had I lied, mostly to myself,
pretending I'd fixed the hour that I would set out?
Three times I reached the door, three times I was called back
as sluggish feet indulged slowed, reluctant heart;
I made those 'final' farewells in my wretchedness,
ran back for one more kiss - the last, I swore, the last.
What else could I do, held fast by love of country?
Yet here it was: the night exile had been decreed.
'Why rush?' I asked again. 'We're headed for the East:
as Carthage was destroyed, Rome must be relinquished.')
Now I felt disengaged, raw, wrenched in two,
limb hacked from limb, bone from bone, sinew from sinew.
In the house, a cry went up, cold, piercing, bereft,
in every corner mourning hands beat on bare breasts
(if I might extrapolate, exchange great for small
such was the sound of defeat, despair at Troy's fall).
My wife clung around my neck as I tried to leave,
our grief intermingled, hearts - and tears - on our sleeves:
'Let me share your journey, an exile's exile wife,
ride stowaway on your departing ship, light freight.
Caesar himself has commanded you to leave here,
for me it's duty, love: love will be my Caesar.'
And so she pleaded, she tried, she tried to persuade
but as so many times before, she tried in vain.
I set out, a corpse too early for its own wake,
carried out for burial, unshaven, unkempt.
My wife fell at our household shrine, faint with sorrow,
half-conscious now, overcome by rising shadow;
lay there calling out my name, moaning in the dust
as if her child - as if I was just laid to rest.

(from *Tristia I.3*)

vi. Malvern Road Station, Cheltenham
I. (9/4/1915)

For once let's not dwell on impending death,
scan the thumbs-up rows of grinning faces
like bone-worn worms grubbing out fresh flesh
for those who got thumbs down, didn't make it -
Wilf Barton, Serge Honey, first from the ship,
returned as cap, belt, identity disc -
a merry bunch, pleased as punch to be off,
that day of fête then cheerful letters home,
spry postcards from a holiday gone wrong:
Aubrey and I drink weak tea now, talk Gloucs,
bullets seem like small birds at dawn chorus...
But back on the platform, between the smiles,
I spot my chap, hesitant, stiff, crowd-shy,
already out with the burying party.

II. (20/1/2005)

I'd hoped for a single snowdrop hunched by the tracks
 - Catullus' flower untouched, as yet, in the grass -
a star-chipped salve to soothe the scar of waste,
stench of rot, not quite sweet, smear of industrial estate.
But there's no hope, no art that can heal the past;
walls have been levelled, diggers come and gone.

The day fails, sky drags with unfallen snow;
the hour, already, of the plough and of the crow.
All we can do here is say nothing and move on.

vii. Burning Books

Take my laurels, such as you've endowed,
for I am a poet no longer:
Unwreathe the ivy from my stone brow;
sadness veins my verse, lines are sorrowed -
my friends, feel it, and then conceal it
as you sigh over my insignia
for you look on the face of exile.
'How many miles,' you say, 'divide us,
our far-dweller friend, comrade Naso.'
Your dedication is most welcome

yet find me now, for better or verse,
only in my ever-changing forms,
mercurial *Metamorphosis*.
Look for quality, though, and not width -
opus interruptus by my flight;
I burnt my books - and my bridges -
on my departure, that last night.
Like Althaea, the worst of mothers,
I destroyed my offspring, my own branch,
sacrificed my undeserving poem,
threw my own entrails on searing pyre.
Did I hate my Muse, my betrayer,
or my own rough work, verse in progress?
(It still survives, of course, is extant:
some copies have been made, so I think.)
I pray it can live for me, be studied
for me, charm for me, remind of me.
Yet who can read it without misgiving
if they don't know revision is missing -
ripped from forge before anvil had finished
not hammered, filed or fine-polished?
So now I don't seek praise but pardon
(for praise will come with patient readers)
offer six new lines for frontispiece:
'Take these orphaned books, give them house-room
grant them, at least, your city's freedom.
Indulge them the more, unedited,
rescued from fire, their parent's death-bed -
the small faults he would have corrected,
all of them, had he been permitted.'

(from *Tristia I.7*)

viii. The Horses

It was all very secret, very hush-hush -
no one knew where they were headed;
the only one who didn't suffer sickness,
my father was in charge of the horses...

A tilted world, Bear tipped upside down
spiralling clouds like splintered spines
and shimmering on the edge of sight
forbidden cities, unknowable lands.
Packed like meat in the stifling hold
he slithered across their sweaty backs
a teetering, punch-drunk charioteer
harnessing terror and then letting go
the reins. Seas reared, distant ranges,
fell, as suddenly, night-dark, star-still,
pebbled, copse-fenced Cotswold pool.

In the late-summer chill of Belgravia
palsied hands paused above a rash of plans:
maybe swords, bayonets, might be enough -
the age-old means of flesh against flesh...

But how can you kill the already dead?
Lined and waiting on the shore
warrior ghosts of three millennia.
Now the only passage through was fear.

Ingeborg Bachmann

Karen Leeder
Introduction to the Life and Writings

INGEBORG BACHMANN was born in 1926 in Klagenfurt, a small Austrian city near what were then the German, Yugoslavian and Italian borders, a place where languages and boundaries had a special significance. Although she published only two collections of poetry before being overtaken by a crisis which led her away from the lyric genre, she is one of the most significant German poets of the twentieth century. Bachmann's arrival on the poetry scene with her first collection, *Die gestundete Zeit* (*Mortgaged time*) in 1953 was a major media event. At the age of 27 she was awarded the coveted prize of the 'Gruppe 47', and a year later the news magazine *Der Spiegel* ran a title story and cover photograph of her. Her initial celebrity had as much to do with her exoticism as with the sense that she gave voice to a particular historical moment. She challenged the expansive consumerist thinking and security of the restorative programmes of the 1950s, by illuminating an altogether darker side of progress.

Don't turn around.
Lace up your shoe.
Chase back the dogs.
Throw the fish in the sea.
Extinguish the lupins.
Harder days are coming.

Bachmann managed to create a new modern poetic language which was at once of its time, yet did not obscure its roots in German tradition. Striking are the many genitive metaphors in which temporal and spatial categories threaten to collapse into one another, the shifting rhythms, the lack of rhymes, and the fusion of abstract language with powerfully concrete images. Her second collection of 1956 *Anrufung des großen Bären* (*Invocation of the Great Bear*) shows a distinct development of her thought. Her relation to the world is more sober and there is an increased preoccupation with language as a subject. In one sense Bachmann had an overwhelming confidence in the utopian potential of the poetic word. This was expressed famously in her poem 'Böhmen liegt am Meer' ('Bohemia lies by the Sea'): 'I border still on a word and on a different land,/I border like little else, on everything more and more'. But she became increasingly aware of the possible contamination of the word and the counterfeit currency of contemporary word-tricksters. Her linguistic scepticism had a philosophical root in her studies of Wittgenstein and Heidegger, and her later poems and her Frankfurt lectures 'Probleme zeitgenössischer Dichtung' ('Problems of Contemporary Poetry') are part of a continuing reflection on the possibilities and inadequacies of language. Amongst her handful of final poems 'Keine Delikatessen' ('No delicacies') of 1963 records a decision to abandon the lyric mode.

Should I
dress up a metaphor
with an almond blossom?
Crucify syntax
on a trick of light?
Who will beat their brains
over such superfluities -

Bachmann did not in fact stop writing poems completely, but shifted her energies into other genres: her short-story collections, radio plays, libretti for Heinz Werner Henze's operas, and especially her first novel *Malina* of 1971, a dark, complex work that was intended as the first part of a trilogy *Todesarten* (*Ways of Dying*). This was never completed: only nine years after she was awarded the prestigious Büchner prize, she died, aged 47, in a fire in her apartment.

Bachmann's antifascist credentials and her commitment to peace are well known. Indeed she was to claim that her childhood came to an end when Hitler and his troops marched triumphantly into the main city square of Klagenfurt. The 'War Diary', published in English here for the first time, is however a far more artless and personal account of war. Far from the elliptical voice most readily associated with Bachmann, one is struck by the directness and simple honesty of the piece; the passions, stubbornness, and humour of a young woman, and her real fear, are all profoundly moving. But one also gets a sense of her literary tastes at this time (Baudelaire, Rilke and Mann) and the philosophical fascination which would lead to her academic career and, one might add, the clarity and precision of her later writing. The five poems are from her literary estate. They were not intended for publication, but they were nevertheless not destroyed, as was the case with many other letters and poems. Although 'William Turner: Gegenlicht', 'Bibliotheken' and 'Wartesaal' have been published in a journal, none of the poems presented here has appeared in English before; and 'Jakobs Ring' and 'Der Gastfreund' appear in German for the first time too. These poems belong to two distinct periods of her life. Although the forensic work that would permit precise dating has not been done, it can safely be assumed that *Jakobs Ring* and *Der Gastfreund* were written in the 1940s, and that the other poems belong to the period of the late 1950s or early 1960s. The critic Hans Höller has made a strong argument that Bachmann's early and late poems are best read together, and indeed without the unifying vision of a discrete creative period associated with a collection, they appear to offer a more transparent commentary on the development of her thought and work. Both early poems suggest a strong biographical frame of reference, although much must remain speculation until more of her biographical writing and correspondence is released for publication - something not expected in my lifetime. What can be said with confidence is that both share the rich, cryptic and archly poetic language of the early period with its frequent mythic reference, and seem to echo works of her fellow poet Paul Celan. The translators argue that the title of 'Jakobs Ring' refers to the complex mandala, the eighteenth minor cycle of which is the Israel cycle. 'Der Gastfreund' makes the characteristic link between love, language and identity in a strikingly sensual diction. The three final poems demonstrate the spare and reduced mode of her later work, which speaks with a greater assurance paradoxically as it assumes a greater intimacy with loss. The loss here is once again of language, intimacy and self. And yet these poems are not totally despairing: the emphasis on light is interesting as in many of the later poems written after the move to Italy, and in two of these at least there is once again a sense of a 'bordering' on life: fingers pointing 'directly at life or at the sky' and 'tracks reaching to the sky'. Finally they bear witness to the painful search for the 'bright words' that will communicate that hope.

Mike Lyons War Diary

INGEBORG BACHMANN'S 'War Diary' covers a period stretching from the late summer of 1944 to June 1945. In September 1944 Ingeborg was an eighteen-year old *Abitur* student at the Klagenfurt high school for girls, known as the Ursulinen-Gymnasium. She lived, mostly alone, in the family's small house in Hensel Street. Her father was an army officer doing war-service in the East and his visits on home leave were infrequent. Since 1943 Ingeborg's mother, her younger sister Isolde and her four-year-old brother Heinz (Heinerle) had been living mainly in the family's other house in Obervellach in the Gail valley, west of Villach and well clear of Klagenfurt with its frequent and increasingly heavy air raids.

At this stage, like many of her contemporaries, Ingeborg faced the prospect of having to do a bazooka training course followed by some form of war-service. As a girl student she could claim exemption by agreeing to do teacher training and signing away her entitlement to higher education. Helped by a family friend, she got a place at the teacher training college. Here the course was dominated by National Socialist ideology, anathema to Ingeborg who was used to the relatively benign atmosphere of the Ursulinen-Gymnasium. Still, her studies at the college continued until early 1945 when, with the collapse of Nazi Germany imminent, and unwilling as she was to go on digging anti-tank ditches, she left the bomb-damaged Klagenfurt house to rejoin the rest of the family in Obervellach.

Her experience at the teacher training college was hardly a catalyst in the development of her anti-Nazism, the foundations of which had already been laid in 1938 when as an eleven-year-old she experienced the trauma of Hitler's annexation of Austria. She was not actually there on 12 March 1938 to see the triumphant entry of German troops into Klagenfurt, but the 'bawling, singing and marching' she found so repellent went on for weeks and left her mind permanently scarred.

In 1944 Mathias Bachmann was badly wounded in east Poland. After hospital treatment and home leave he returned to the front only to be caught up in the German collapse outside Prague. Avoiding capture by the Red Army, he surrendered to the Americans and was soon, probably in August 1945, back home in Obervellach. Unable because of his Nazi past to resume his teaching career, he nevertheless decided to finance the university education of his two daughters by mortgaging the Obervellach house. So it was that at the end of 1945 Ingeborg was able to start her studies in Innsbruck and later continue them in Vienna.

The manuscript contains references to persons who, for good reasons, are not identified by name. The Bachmann family wish to maintain this discretion.

Confusingly, only the later entries in the diary are properly dated.

Issi is one of Ingeborg's school-friends and not be confused with Isi, her sister Isolde.

In the rhetorical flourish at the start of the third paragraph Ingeborg is recalling these lines from Rilke's *Book of Hours*: 'Was wirst du tun, Gott, wenn ich sterbe?/Ich bin dein Krug (wenn ich zerscherbe?)/Ich bin dein Trank (wenn ich verderbe?)/ Bin dein Gewand und dein Gewerbe,/mit mir verlierst du deinen Sinn.'

Ali was the neighbours' dog.

Ingeborg is rightly dismissive of the suggestion that the acronym FSS might point to a link with the Secret Service. It stands for Field Security Section. Field Security was a branch of the Army Intelligence Corps and was concerned in Austria with denazification, frontier control and the gathering of intelligence.

The questionnaire completed by Ingeborg was standard and designed to establish whether the interviewee had been a member of the Nazi Party or any of its subsidiaries, including of course the League of German Girls (*BDM: Bund Deutscher Mädel*). The latter, affiliated to the Hitler Youth (*Hitler Jugend*), had as its mission the National Socialist upbringing of girls between the ages of 14 and 21.

Jews with backgrounds like that of Jack Hamesh were numerous in Field Security. By defying local anti-Semitic bigots and maintaining her friendship with Jack, Ingeborg showed great courage. After his demob she kept in touch with him till 1946/47 when he is thought to have emigrated to Palestine.

War Diary

DEAR diary, I've been rescued. I don't have to go to Poland or do bazooka training. Daddy was here and went with me from Vellach to Klagenfurt; he went to see Dr Hasler, who advised him to get me signed up straightaway at the teacher training college, for teachers are in short supply. I could never even have dreamt that one day the detested teacher training college would be my salvation. I was immediately registered and enrolled as a final year student, on a fast-track course, and you have to teach while still being taught yourself. Everything went smoothly at the Regional Office. The only nasty bit was being seen by the assessor for girls doing teacher training and so exempt from war-service under the emergency scheme. I was there twice, the first time she wasn't there, I could scarcely recall her or her face, All I remember was her making the dreadful pronouncement that I would have to behave myself, otherwise it would be all up with me in spite of my good report. And that she said 'Mädel' with a very long 'ä'. This time too she tried to appeal to my better nature, but I got in there first, since I knew from talking to Hasler what line to take and I said I was sure now I wasn't of degree calibre and so I wanted to be a teacher, also because for the war-effort teaching children was more important - and I added: for the children too. That shut her up. The only thing was I knew you had to sign a form declaring under oath that you were renouncing any claim to a university education. I hesitated for a moment and then I signed. No, I am sure that in this country I shall never continue my studies, not with this war still going on. What madness to hesitate even for an instant! Today we had the first lesson at school. I was almost glad to be back again. But can you call it school? I think the girls in my class are all fanatics. After the first lesson the air-raid warning went and that was that. But Wilma - she used to be in my class - is also on the course. She did the same thing as me. She didn't come with me, but biked over to Annabichl and then home, and so now here I am, stretched out at our favourite spot by the edge of the forest. Issi brought the flour mush from the chemist's and we're fetching water from the stream to stir into it. Sunshine. She's asleep, sunning herself. After five hours still no all-clear. Still no bombs. Once a couple of fighter-bombers came in low and fired a burst or two ...

The Russians are in Vienna and probably already somewhere in Styria. I have talked it all over with Issi. It is not at all simple. She doesn't know whether she can get something out of the poisons cupboard. We are both scared of the Russians. Of course, I don't believe everything I'm told, but no one can foretell what they will do with us, whether they will leave us here or take us to Siberia. You have to expect the worst.

What will you do, God, if I die …. I'm not going up into the shelter again. The Tschörners are already dead and a day later, Ali also met his end. Our Ali. There is nobody left in the street. The days are so sunny. I've put a chair in the garden and I read. I've made up my mind to go on reading when the bombs are falling. *The Book of Hours* is already crumpled and messy. It is a great comfort to me. And Baudelaire! Bientot nous tomberons dans les froides tenebres, adieu vive clarte. I no longer need to look at the book. Yesterday we had the biggest raid ever. The first formation flew over, the second dropped its bombs. The droning noise was so powerful that it took my breath away and then I did go down into the basement, which in our little house was ridiculous as it wouldn't withstand even a small bomb, let alone one weighing 100 kg. They say it looks terrible in the city, and even here it's like the end of the world. But I'm not scared, only when the bombs fall there's this physical sensation, a sort of stomach cramp. But in my mind I have made my will. Maybe it's sinful just to stay sitting there, staring into the sun. But I cannot go into the shelter for hours at a time, with the water running down the rock walls and the air so bad that you nearly faint. There is a ban on talking because of the air, but the silence of those abject masses of people is unbearable too. The thought of perishing with them like cattle is dreadful. At least let it be in the garden. In the sun.

This morning A. said we're not allowed out any more when the air-raid warning goes. He's like a madman. This morning he saw that Wilma was wearing her little silver pendant with its crucifix and was so enraged that he nearly threw her downstairs. At 7 o'clock tomorrow we all have to go out into the Annabichl fields to dig trenches. 'Klagenfurt must be defended to the last man and to the last woman,' he bawled. I immediately talked the matter over with Wilma. She has to join her brothers and sisters. They have been bombed out and their mother is in bed somewhere, dreadfully ill. I shall go there on my own and see how things are and, if need be, invent some excuse for her. Issi, dear sweet Issi, consoled me. We went again to the edge of the wood and in the end even had a laugh. The 'cover supremo' was there again, crawling around in the bushes 20 metres from us like a startled weasel. Whenever low-flying aircraft strafed the trains he stuck his head out of the bushes, shouting hysterically, 'Take cover, ladies! Take cover, ladies!' And Issi, who nearly chokes when she can't stop laughing, finally gasped and said, 'What a well brought-up young man!' Then she told me the latest jokes from the chemist's and we had cold potatoes. Tomorrow we must really be on our toes.

All the kids were there to do the shovelling, but not a single member of staff. Nor A., needless to say. The prefects were in charge of course, and anyway no one in this flock of sheep showed any awareness of the effrontery of our role-models, the teachers. In my rage I poked around with my shovel in the hard ground. I didn't feel at all ill but must have looked quite pale, because half an hour later the girl next to me said, 'Are you feeling sick?' I mumbled something indistinct and kept thinking to myself what they are doing to us cries out to heaven. The adults, our esteemed 'mentors' who want to get us killed. When the alarm went some of the younger ones got agitated, far and wide no houses or cellars, and all those factories in the vicinity. Nearby there was a wooden shed and a bomb-damaged nursery garden. My bike was there and I said I needed to sit down for a bit. As ill luck would have it a short while before a few older Hitler Youth Leaders turned up to check the trenches, yelling 'Get on with it!' In spite of that I got away, leaned against the side of the shed and, since no one could see me properly, jumped on the bike and rode off. Bombs were already falling in Pischeldorf Street. I lay down in an old crater in the meadow and then half an hour later went to call on Wilma.

Wilma seems calmer. The two of us are not going back to school. In any case we are not yet known to all the teachers. A. probably doesn't know me at all. And Hasler definitely won't say anything. Wilma is afraid we could be shot as deserters. But in all this turmoil I think we can rule out any chance of people bothering about us.

In the cellar I have got together the most important things. I'll take them with me to the Gailtal when the time comes. But for now I shall stay here. I found Liselotte in a box. I put her into her frilly pink dress and she is lying in bed with me. She can't say 'Mama' any more, and neither can I. Oh, Mummy, Mummy! And Heinerle, my angel. No post. Nothing.

Talking to the grown-ups has become pointless.

EVERYONE living within ten kilometres of the frontier needs a pass. Vellach is still within the frontier zone. If you want a pass or are looking for a job you have to go to the FSS. I don't know what that means, lots of them say 'Secret Service', but of course that's nonsense. I was there today and it was quickly my turn. There were two Englishmen in the office, one of them really wild-looking, with a beard; he's said to be from South Africa. The other is small and a bit ugly, glasses, speaks German fluently with a Viennese accent. The South African speaks it worse, very haltingly. The little one made me fill in a questionnaire, then he looked at it and said: 'So you've done your matric.' I think he was surprised because all the others are peasant girls. Then he said: 'BDM, of course.' Suddenly I felt quite sick and couldn't say a word and just nodded. I could have told him that I am probably no longer listed, because I didn't join at 14, never even took the oath, and later too never got roped in or went along of my own accord. But I don't know what came over me. I thought too they probably all tell him they were never members or only because they were forced, and straightaway I also thought he wouldn't believe a word of it. Finally, he said 'Think again very carefully about whether you were a leader or not. We're bound to find out if you were.' I managed to say 'No'. But I believe I turned quite red and in desperation even redder. Why you should turn red and tremble when you are telling the truth is beyond me.

Yesterday I enquired about my pass. The South African was the only one there so I'll have to go back; it will take me a day or two to get the pass. Close to the local government offices, by the greengrocer's, the other one suddenly got off a bike. He still remembered my name and was totally changed, no longer sarcastic, embarrassed rather. His name is Jack Hamesh. I was quite embarrassed too. He asked me where I live in Vellach and he walked with me as far as the bridge. I don't know why he wanted to talk to me. He asked if Uncle Christl is related to me, and of course I said 'Yes', adding that just about everybody called Bachmann is related to us. Why Uncle Christl ended up in a camp, when it was the Gs and the Ms who were the most fanatical Nazis, I don't know; everybody thinks that the Gs, who own the only shops in the village, must be behind all this. Now they are all denouncing one another, especially the Nazis as a group, because they all think that this way they can get off lightly. Of course I didn't say a word about what I thought, he would definitely not have understood and after all I scarcely know him. I don't know either what he wants from me.

11 June. L. has fallen in love with an Englishman, he is tremendously tall and gangling and is called Bob. She says he is very rich and was brought up in Oxford. He's all she can talk about. Yesterday she said she had just one wish, to get away from here and go to England. She's hoping, I think, that he will marry her. But marriage between Austrian girls and Englishmen is prohibited by the military government. She says the hardships here will never end and that she has gone through too much, can't take any more, and wants a life for herself. I can understand her only too well but get angry with her too, because she thinks I also ought to marry an Englishman and get away from here. Of course I want to get away, but only in order to study, and I don't want to get married and not even to an Englishman, just for the sake of a few tins of food and some silk stockings. Most of the Englishmen here are very nice and decent, I think. But I am much too young. Arthur and Bill are really very nice and we talk and laugh a lot together. In the garden we often play Tailor, Tailor, Lend Me Your Scissors and Look Behind You. Arthur keeps giving Heinerle chocolate, and a few days ago he called on Mummy, who is still in bed, and put tea and biscuits onto her bedspread. She calls him 'Redilocks', because he has such ginger hair, and likes him best. I think he also is in love with L., Bill is too, but Arthur more so, and I think too that Arthur is terribly jealous of Bob. Bob is quite standoffish. We once exchanged a couple of words but never again and even then it didn't amount to much: it was just to thank him for letting L. have the car so that she could fetch Mummy from hospital.

14 June. My mind is in a whirl still. Jack Hamesh was here again, this time he came in a jeep. Everyone in the village was gawping of course and S. came across the stream twice to look into the garden. I took him into the garden because Mummy is in bed upstairs. We sat on the bench and to begin with I was trembling again so badly that he must have thought I was mad or had something on my conscience or whatever. And I just don't know why. I no longer know what we talked about first, but then all at once it was about books, about Thomas Mann and Stefan Zweig and Schnitzler and Hofmannsthal. I was so happy, he knows everything, and he told me he would never have thought he might meet a young girl in Austria who in spite of her Nazi upbringing had read all that. And suddenly everything was quite different, and I told him all about the books. He told me that he was taken to England in 1938 in a *Kindertransport* with other Jewish children. Actually he was already 18 years old at the time, but an uncle managed to arrange it, his parents were already dead. Now I know too why he speaks such good German. Then he joined the British army and in the occupation zones lots of former Germans and Austrians are now working in the offices of the FSS, on account of the language and because they know the conditions in the country better. We talked till evening, and he kissed my hand before he left. Nobody ever kissed my hand before. I am so mixed up and happy, and when he'd gone I climbed the apple tree in our garden, it was already dark, and I cried my eyes out and thought to myself that I would never wash my hand again.

Jack comes every day now, and I've never talked so much in my life. We talk mostly about *Weltanschauung* and history. He's very good at explaining, and I'm no longer in the least embarrassed by him. I always ask him if it's something I haven't yet heard about. At the moment we're doing socialism and communism (and of course if Mummy were to hear the word 'communism' she would faint!), but you must have detailed knowledge of everything and study. I'm reading Marx's *Capital* and a book by Adler. I've told Jack that I'd like to study philosophy, and he takes me very seriously and thinks that is right for me. But I've kept quiet about the poems.

L. has borrowed my shoes, because of Bob. I'm happy to lend them to her now and then, but now she's wearing them all the time and I have to go around in my old house shoes, even when Jack comes. Mummy thinks that's very inconsiderate of her. Jack thinks she is very clever and she calls round sometimes if she's got time, then it's more fun. I think that like everyone else he likes her, but I don't mind. You can't talk sensibly to her at all now, she's up there in the clouds. I begin to doubt if she will ever be a good doctor, for dancing and having a good time and flirting are much more important for her. She is quite changed. I think also that her father is worried. Bob has given her a car, and so now she has two, an official Red Cross car and one of her own, and Bill, who has gone all moody, often acts as her chauffeur and drives her around. He is so naïve and kind.

So that's the way things are. They are all talking about me and of course that goes for all my relatives too. 'She's going out with that Jew.' And Mummy is quite tense because of all the gossip, and she can't understand what it all means for me! She avoids the subject and so today when we were cooking, I brought it up and told her nothing is ever said between us that could not be heard by a third person, that she herself must know this and was best able to sense it herself. After all, she knows me! But it's not about that but about 'me and the Jew'. And I told her that I shall walk up and down through Hermagor and Vellach with him ten times in a row and if that upsets them, so much the better.

This is the loveliest summer of my life, and if I live to be a hundred this spring and summer will still be the loveliest. 'Not much real sign of peace' is what they all say, but for me peace is peace! People are so terribly stupid. Did they really expect that such a catastrophe would be followed by some kind of earthly paradise? That the British would have nothing better on their minds than making our lives a bed of roses? Goodness me, even a few months ago who would have thought that we would even survive? Now I can go up the Goria again every day, just to be alone and dream, how marvellous to dream! I shall study, work, write! I am alive, I am alive. My God, to be free and alive, even without shoes, without bread and butter, without stockings, without .... Oh, what more can I say? This is a splendid time!

We don't talk about Daddy any more. I don't, because of Mummy, and she doesn't, because of us. If only he had really been in Prague ... Jack says that the Americans and the British are already releasing lots of prisoners, but of course nothing is known about the Russians. Basically nothing at all is known. From Vienna there are rumours of looting and rape, it's awful. Shall I be able to get to Vienna at all? When? How? I can't stay here for ever, waiting and waiting. There is nothing for me to do here, nothing to learn. If the universities don't open soon. I'll have to look for a job. Maybe with the British, so that we have something to eat. There is less and less. Yesterday we got our ration of horse meat and two of the three tins were bad. Thank goodness for Aunty Rosa! So we do at least have milk for Heinerle, but already he looks like a tiny skeleton. I don't understand it, for we're doing all we can for him.

Patrick Drysdale and Mike Lyons Five Bachmann Poems

Jakobs Ring

Platanen, von Kälte umgürtet, waren zugegen,
straffer zog auch der Wind mein Kleid vor den Toren,
und du riefst mich ins Haus, wo du zur Nacht warst befohlen.

Diesseits und jenseits des Rheins blieben die Fenster geschlossen,
und wir öffneten eins, um im Finstern zu hoffen
über dem Ring deines Volks, das sie im Wasser begruben.

Hüllt ich dich ein? Du solltest die Brücken nicht sehen,
in die Wolken gesprengt und in Stücke gerissen.
Frag: so täuschtest du mich und den Ring vor den Toten?

Uferwärts heim in der Verfolgung neuer Gezeiten
trug ich den Ring, er sprach für dein künftiges Leben:
es freie fortan kein Wind das Laub der Platanen,

es breche kein Aug mehr, das tiefer sieht als die andern,
und Israels Kinder soll kein Wasser berühren.

Jacob's Wheel

Plane trees, encircled by cold, stood there before me,
wind at the gates pulled my dress more tightly about me,
and you called me into the house where you were sent for the night-time.

This side and that of the Rhine, the windows stayed shuttered;
we opened one up in order to hope in the darkness
over the wheel of your people, those who were buried in water.

Did I enfold you? You were meant not to notice the bridges,
those blown up to the clouds and ripped into pieces.
Ask: so you cheated both me and the wheel in front of the dead ones?

Going home along banks in pursuit of new tideways,
I carried the wheel, it spoke for your life in the future;
so from now on let no wind woo the leaves of the plane trees,

let no eye ever break that observes more deeply than others,
and the children of Israel shall be untouched by water.

Der Gastfreund

Manchmal kommt Einer
aus fremdem Land,
fremd gekleidet,
mit fremder Zunge.
Doch wie man Ihm in die Augen sieht,
begreift man,
dass Er begreift.
Man lehnt den Kopf an Seine Schulter
und beginnt Dinge zu erzählen
nach denen Er nie fragen würde:
dass einem der Wind bis ans Herz schlägt,
dass man die Sterne bis ins Blut spürt,
dass man...
Er steht, hört und versteht.
Man kann die ganze Brust an die Seine geben,
die Arme um Ihn schlingen...
Und so hat man Ihn,
hat sich,
bis zur Mitternacht!

The Visitor

At times Someone comes
from a strange land,
strangely dressed,
with a strange tongue.
Yet when you look Him in the eye,
you comprehend
that He comprehends.
You lean your head against his shoulder
and begin to speak of things
about which He would never ask:
That the wind strikes right into your heart,
that you feel the stars right into your blood,
that you . . .
He stands, hears and understands.
You can press your whole body against His,
wrap your arms around Him . . .
And so you have Him,
have yourself,
until midnight!

Bibliotheken

Die Bücherborde biegen sich.
Die Bände lasten von Vergangenheit.
Ihr Schweiss ist Staub.
Ihre Regung ist Starre.
Sie kennen keinen Kampf mehr.
Sie haben sich gerettet
auf die Insel des Wissens.
Manche haben dabei das Gewissen verloren.
Stellenweise aber ragen
Menschenfinger aus ihnen
und weisen geradewegs in das Leben
oder in den Himmel.

Libraries

The bookshelves sag,
the volumes burdened with the past.
Their sweat is dust,
their sensation numbness.
They know no further struggle.
They have escaped
to the Island of Knowledge.
Some have thus lost their conscience.
But here and there people's fingers
stick out of them
and point directly at life
or at the sky.

William Turner: Gegenlicht

Über ein Land mit sparsamer Sonne
spannte er seine Leinwand und streifte
die Wege nah an den Himmel.
Er wusste:
es kommt auf den Lichteinfall an.

Von sich selbst hielt er wenig
und erlaubte sich keine Perspektiven

William Turner: Backlight

Across a land with meagre sun
he stretched his canvas and brushed in
the tracks reaching to the sky.
He knew:
it depends on the fall of light.

To himself he gave little thought
and allowed himself no perspectives.

Wartezimmer

Die Sprache verbindet nicht mehr.
Gemeinsam ist uns das Warten.
Ein Stuhl
eine Bank
ein Fenster
durch das das Licht in unser Zimmer
fällt
auf unsere Hände
auf unsere Augen
und sonst
auf den Boden.

Heile unsere Augen
damit wir wieder Worte finden
bunte, die ich dir sagen kann.

Waiting Room

Language no longer unites.
What we share is waiting.
A chair
a bench
a window
through which light falls
into our room
onto our hands
onto our eyes
and also
onto the floor.

Heal our eyes
so that we again find words,
bright ones that I can say to you.

The translators gratefully acknowledge the helpful advice they had from Karen Leeder in their work on these poems.

Sean O'Brien: A version of Canto V of Dante's *Inferno*

Working on the Inferno

THE *Inferno*, we are told, is the most frequently translated work of European poetry. This is hardly surprising, but it begs the question of why anyone should undertake to add to the mountain. All I can say is that the poem is fascinating, poignant, terrifying, beautiful and strange, and that in order to try to understand it better I have been working on a version of my own while hoping that readers might find it has something to add to the existing array of translations. What I have wanted to suggest is, firstly, the pungent, dank, abrasive physical immediacy of Hell, with its lakes, towers, graveyards, cliffs, ruins and insanely ingenious prison-castellations, its vast, minutely inventive programmes of torture, its swarming population of demons and damned souls. I have never read a version of the *Inferno* that was not interesting, but I have at times felt that the glare and heat of Hell have been diminished - an experience akin to watching an old print of a film. Perhaps this has something to do with ideas of fidelity which are more likely to preserve the poem than to reveal it. In attempting to write equivalents to *terza rima* there is an obvious danger that the poem will be sacrificed to the success of rhyme. The English thus produced may belong in a kind of translatorial limbo, unable to cross over into the realm of plausible usage. What is impassioned may become merely strenuous; what is particular and concrete may appear merely generic. One way of trying to avoid this is to work in blank verse, with its enormous flexibility, momentum, weight, pace and grandeur, and its congruence with the human voice. The choice of form is, of course, intended as a tribute to the original.

Canto V

In darkness we descended to the next
Grim circle: here the space is more confined,
The pain intensified in goaded howls.

And here King Minos serves as magistrate:
Assessing the offences of the damned,
He judges and dispatches each in turn.

Believe me, friends, arraigned before this bench
The malefactors instantly confess -
And when the Justice-King has heard their crimes,

He knows the place where each of them belongs
And coils his tail around himself to show
How many levels they must now descend.

The court of Minos never sleeps. The crowd
Awaiting sentence never thins. They speak;
They learn their fate; and they are hurled below.

'Now, visitor to this, the house of pain,'
Said Minos, seeing me and looking up
A moment from his stern, unceasing work,

'Beware this entranceway. Think whom you trust.
And though the door is wide, do not be fooled.'
Then Virgil came to my defence: 'Enough.

You may not interfere. The road this man
Must follow is his destiny, laid down
By Him who wills all things. Now hold your tongue.'

Just then the notes of grief began to reach
My hearing, and I came to where in waves
Vast choirs of agony broke over me.

This was a place where light itself was dumb.
It held the roar the sea builds in a storm
When two opposing winds contend, a storm

Which cannot cease, since it is brewed in Hell.
It snatches sinners up and hurls them on
Before it, spins them, whips them. Tortured souls

In this unending fury screech aloud
In pain and tears and lamentation - yet
In that same breath they curse the might of God.

I learned this is a penalty reserved
For those whose sins are of the flesh, who seek
To make the reason subject to desire.

As in cold weather starlings' wings will bear
A broad dense flock of them along, so here
The storm conducts the spirits of the damned:

Here, there, downwards, upwards, on they go:
No hope will ever come to comfort them,
No moment's rest, and no reprieve from pain.

Now when I saw these shadows veering close,
Borne on the warring winds eternally,
Like flocks of cranes strung out against the sky,

Delivering their mournful, long-drawn cries,
I asked my master, 'Can you tell me, please,
Who are these souls the very air torments?'

'The first of those whose names are known to you,'
He said, 'could once command a hundred tongues.
She was an Empress, but one so depraved

By her indulgence in the fleshly sins
That she enshrined her lust among her laws
To mock the scandal that pursued her deeds.

Her name was Semiramis and we read
How she succeeded to her husband's throne
And ruled the land which now the Sultan holds.

See Dido next, who killed herself for love
And broke faith with Sichaeus' memory;
And Cleopatra, Egypt's wanton queen.

And here is Helen, too, in whose account
Stand years of evil; great Achilles
Fought with love and found no quarter there.

See Paris, Tristan...' Then he pointed out
A thousand shades and more who died for love,
And as he did so named them each in turn.

To hear my teacher catalogue these names,
The knights and ladies of the ancient world,
Awoke first pity, then bewilderment.

I asked him, 'Poet, may I be allowed
To speak to these two fellow travellers,
Who seem to ride so lightly on the wind?'

'Wait. Let them come closer,' he replied,
'And then invoke the love that leads them on:
They will accept your invitation then.'

So when the tempest drove them near to us
I called to them: 'O weary souls, if God
Wills that you may, please come to speak to us.'

As doves when summoned by desire will seek
Their nest with poised and outstretched wings,
Borne down the sky by longing, so these two

Left the company that Dido leads,
Approaching us through that malignant air:
My tender voice was powerful indeed.

'O gracious, friendly human creature,
Who travels through this filthy atmosphere
To meet us, though we stained the world with blood,

If that great friend of all were still our friend
Then we should pray to him to grant you peace
For taking pity on our dreadful plight.

Whatever matters you would speak about,
Or hear about from us, this place is best,
For here the wind relents a little now.

The city of my birth lies on the shore
At which the River Po and all the streams
That feed its course descend to meet the sea.

The fire of love is quickly kindled in
A gentle heart, and I burned for the one
Snatched from me. I am burning still.

The power of love spares nobody its claims:
Its charms imprisoned me so utterly
That as you see, I shall not be released.

And it was love that brought us to this death.
The pit of Cain awaits our killer now.'
So with these words the lost pair greeted us.

I heard these words and had to bend my head,
Unable to go on, until at last
The poet said to me, 'What are your thoughts?'

When finally I spoke I said: 'Alas,
What sweet thoughts and what intense desire
Brought this couple to their dreadful fate.'

I turned towards them then and searched for words:
'Francesca, what you suffer makes me weep
With sorrow and compassion. Please, explain

How, in the midst of sighs and sweetness, love
Could give you signs, then opportunity
To satisfy your dark forbidden wish?'

She answered me: 'No greater pain exists
Than to be damned and still remember joy.
Your master-poet understands this too.

But if you are determined you must hear
About the root of our forbidden love
Then I shall tell, and weep in doing so.

One day, to entertain ourselves, we read
Of Lancelot, bound hand and foot by love.
We sat alone. There seemed no danger then.

Our eyes met many times as we read on.
The drama made us blush and then grow pale.
It was a single line that ruined us -

When we read how a long-desired smile
Was kissed by that great lover, then my own
True love, the one from whom I'll never part,

Reached out for me, and, trembling, kissed my mouth.
The pander Galahad devised that work:
That afternoon we set his book aside.'

While one unhappy spirit spoke these words
The other wept and I was overcome
By pity, and I fainted clean away

And like a dead man fell upon the ground.

Christina Viti: Eros Alesi's *Fragments*

EROS ALESI (1951-1971) is the author of a brief and fragmented diary
which at first glance some readers might be inclined to dismiss as noth-
ing more than one young man's confession; but growing up in and
around European cities in the Sixties were thousands of young people
who had come to a starkly simple conclusion: if life (or 'tae choose life'
as Irvine Welsh would put it) means nothing but drudgery and crushed
expectations, then death is preferable. In its raw immediacy, Alesi's
account of his shipwrecked search for a new, adult identity paints a much
more accurate portrait of life in metropolitan Italy than most would sus-
pect, and shows the beginnings of an awareness of poetic form.

Alesi belonged to the generation that was introduced to the concept of
derangement as a pathway to self-knowledge and spirituality by the works
of what we have reductively come to know as the Beat writers. Allen
Ginsberg's *Hydrogen Jukebox*, translated into Italian by Fernanda Pivano
and published in 1965, had jump-started a revolution in poetic language
that seemed connected through huge feedback loops to changes in the
perception of the self.

I think a close look at Alesi's *Fragments* will show how deep that influ-
ence was: on the existential level, it took the form of an involvement with
Oriental philosophies and the positing of communes as an alternative to
the nuclear family; on the structural level, it is interesting to note the
echoing of stanzas in the first section of *Howl*, introduced by the relative
pronoun 'who', with paragraphs in the *Fragments* separated by the con-
junction 'that' (the Italian for both words is *che*).

Similarities are also found in imagery ('the destructo-creative machine
of the universe', 'thriceshivers', 'the goddess and ungoddess death'), and
in the addressing of the poem directly to the author's late parent, remi-
niscent, it seems to me, of the poignancy of Ginsberg's *Kaddish*.

Paradoxically, it is precisely this limit that lifts Alesi's work above the
mere jottings of a strung-out boy: conscious imitation of an extant poet-
ic form as an attempt to code one's destruction and so transcend it.

Poetry exists because the heart rebels against the suppression of its
inner life. Whether Alesi, had he survived addiction and crime, would
have gone on to strengthen his own voice and to articulate rebelliousness
in a more complex form is for the reader to decide; but I think few can
fail to recognize in his work the courage to follow the introspective jour-
ney without which writing is doomed to irrelevance.

Fragments (1971)

Dear Dad.

You who are now in the heavenly pastures, in the earthly pastures, in the marine pastures.
You who are in the human pastures. You who vibrate in the air. You who still love your son Alesi Eros.
You who have wept for your son. You who follow his life with your vibrations past and present.
You who are loved by your son. You who solely existed in him. You who are called dead, ash, garbage.
You who are for me my protecting shadow.
You who at this moment I love and feel closer than anything else.
You who are and will be my life's photocopy.

That I was 6 or 7 when I saw you Handsome - strong - proud - assured - daring respected and feared by others, that I was 10 or 11 when I saw you violent, absent, bad, that I saw you as the ogre that I judged you a Bastard because you beat my mum.
That I was 13 or 14 when I saw you saw yourself losing your role.
That I saw you saw the rise of my new role, of my mother's new role.
That I was 15 and a half when I saw you saw the gallons of wine and bottles of brandy increasing at a frightening rate.
That I saw you saw the look in your eyes was no longer handsome, strong, proud, upright, respected and feared by others.
That I saw you saw my mother growing distant. That I saw you saw the beginning of an ordinary tragic undoing.
That I saw you saw the gallons of wine and bottles of brandy increasing at a great rate.
That I was 15 and a half that I saw you saw that I was running away from home, that my mother was running away from home.
That you wanted to play Tough.
That you did not stop anyone.
That you ended up alone in a self-contained two-bedroom flat.
That the gallons of wine and bottles of brandy kept increasing.
That one day. That the day. You came to pick me up from the police station cells in Milan I saw you saw yourself alone. That you wanted either your wife or your son or both in that self-contained two-bed-room flat. That I saw you saw you would do anything to have that back.
That I saw you saw your hand stretched out in a gesture of peace, an armistice.
That I saw you saw a gob of spit on your hand.

That I saw you saw your eyes weeping solitude caked with punitive, masochistic blood.

That I saw. That you saw the desire to punish your life.

That I saw you saw the desire not to suffer. That I saw you saw the gallons of wine and bottles of brandy kept on increasing.

That I saw you saw at that time your future life.

That I knew you knew that your son was an addict that your wife was carrying another man's child (the child she would not give you).

That I saw you saw 3 years go by. That I saw you saw that on 09/12/69 you did not come to visit me in the madhouse. Because you had died.

That now you see I see. That now you are the first that you play this dead man's hand as the dead man.

But that you play anyway, that now you see I see that I worship you that I love you from the depths of my being.

That now you see I see that my mother thinks ruefully of. ALESI FELICE FATHER OF ALESI EROS.

That now you see I see that I have once again fled towards solitude.

That you see I see only vast huge blackness the same blackness I saw you saw.

That now you will continue to see what I see.

*

That dear father I will tell you about my journey to India. That I am sure, certain you are listening.

That it's been several months on amphetamines. That at a certain point amphetamines were impossible to find in chemists'. That the black market was extortionate. That my journey to Naples - return ticket - that Naples was almost a virgin market for amphetamines. That the return ticket to Rome ended up in a toilet. That one month in Naples, a city that wants to move with the times albeit retaining an unnoticeable traditionalism - that in Naples, Piazza Municipio, there was Gionata Usi, Lorens and many others. That everyday two three bottles of Ritalin-Metredrina-Desoxyn-Psichergina-Tempodex. That then the chance of a ten thousand lire theft and my obsessive paranoia brought me to Foggia - that escape to Manfredonia - that the only hippy in Manfredonia gives me his ID card - that I hitch-hike on to Brindisi - that your spirit, your words, your molecules helped me along. That I find five thousand lire enough to sail to Gominizza - that then father nothing, no hypodermics no intravenous. That I just travelled mostly on foot, on the hairpin bends of the mountains that are Salonica's dividing line. That in Salonica I met with a Frenchman ripe for a just and unjust revenge. That dear dad he was ripe for goddess and ungoddess death. That he returned to France that I was heading for Istanbul.

That dear father Istanbul reminds us - reminds me of a year in jail.
That dear father I love you and have nearly always loved you. That I did
not want your anxiety, your grief. That I arrive in Istanbul with a faked
ID card, without a Turkish penny. That I steal two passports, an amaz-
ing watch and some loose change. That in Istanbul I was injecting
immemorable doses of opium tincture. That I was serene, that I wasn't
thinking of you except in short bursts. That after the theft an obsessive
paranoia. That a taxi to Eastern Istanbul. That paranoia was corroding
me. That at last Izmit. That I meet a Frenchman on his maiden voyage.
That I work in Modino thanks to my knowledge of Turkish. That one
afternoon from inside a fourth-class hotel. That here George
Souterbanc leaves his trousers containing passport and two hundred
and fifty dollars at the foot of the bed. That dear father great
introspective struggle. That in the end I flee with the Frenchman's
trousers. That a taxi. That 50 grams of liquid opium. That a village
whose name I don't remember I take a bus heading for Ankara. That
obsessive paranoia. That in Ankhara plane to Erzurum. That hours
counted through a dropper. That finally heading for Iran. That three
days travelling drinking the stomach-turning liquid of liquid opium.
That first stop the customs, and my opium safe. That then Tabriz, a few
hours' rest. That dates and apples I bought. That finally Tehran. That
Amircabir Hotel the moneyed tourists' Hotel. That opium and heaps.
That heroin five times, smoked, as per local custom. That sniffing - that
fixing. That I was expecting more from the queen of drugs. That
twenty 32 mg. morphine tablets. That chillum. That counting. That a
new theft (transistor watch) that less paranoia than the first time. That a
train for Mescad. That the last pennies for Herat (Afghanistan). That in
Herat help because of reciprocated liking for a German kid. That
travelling to Kandar I meet an old French companion, Franswas. That
together we eke it out on the last money I've left from the petty little
theft of a few vials of morphine.
That the self was travelling. That the self was reduced to colourful rags.
That the bells were tolling. That they were tolling 12, slowly. That I would
love to drink a glass of cold milk.

*

Dear, sweet, good, humane, sociable mother morphine. That you only
you sweetest mother morphine have loved me like I wanted. You loved
me whole. I am the fruit of your blood. That you only you succeeded in
making me feel secure. That you succeeded in giving me the quantity of
happiness indispensable to my survival. That you gave me a home, a
hotel, a bridge, a train, a doorway, I accepted them, that you gave me the
whole friendly universe.

That you gave me a social role, that requests and gives. That at 15 I accepted to live as a 'man' human being only because you were there, you who offered yourself to create me anew. That you taught me to take my first steps. That I learnt my first words. That I felt the first pains of my new life. That I felt the first pleasures of my new life. That I learnt to live as I had always dreamt I would live. That I learnt to live under your care, the numberless attentions of mother morphine. That I will never be able to renege my past with mother morphine. That gave me so much. That saved me from a suicide or a madness that had all but destroyed my life jacket.

That today 22/12/1970 I can scream out once again to myself, to others, to all that is noble strength, that nothing and nobody ever gave me as much as my benefactor, adopter, mother morphine. That you are boundless love boundless charity. That I will leave you only when I am mature for my friend death or when I can rely on my own strength enough to be able to stand without mother morphine's powerful vitamins.

*

That you through all the streets and alleys in the world, that I either in a madhouse or a jail of whatever city in the world.
That twice this sad reality posited itself and both times I have run to your magical and mysterious home, the Orient and both times I have embraced you again with all the love you have taught me to have.

*

That I am fresh out of the madhouse a third time, a third enforced separation from you MOTHER MORPHINE. That I am sure, that I am almost sure, that before long I will be embracing you again.
That two thirty of 23rd December 1970 people talking about my search, search only I have engaged in that only I and mother morphine know, that only I and she have continued in the search for new truths mine and for me like the truth I love Giorgio. Like the truth of two who are looking in the other room for someone to impersonify him.
That I'm in touch with Giorgio.
That I felt Ettore go down and I don't like to be the sole winner that I am terrified of ending up alone, under any condition. But that I have to be alone to become Buddha.
That at 4.10 I heard Ettore's voice loudly and clearly implicating me in his grief. That Giorgio's voice pointed to the truth.
That at 4.20 in Piazza Bologna me and the essence, the memory, the impression of Giorgio gave the others one big gob of spit. Because they

were not like us. That in a while the Bonaventura family will find the dear little warmth it seeks in a bed in the house on via Andrea Fulvio. That I want no wounded.

*

That the commune of via Andrea Fulvio contributed to the formation of my defence army. Army that has to defend itself from its own state. That the commune, like the fact I was expelled from India and like many other facts screamed out to me that the enemy I identified, and perhaps still identify, with other living beings was nothing but my own self. That perhaps at this point I could say that my flight my insisting upon my role, my journey turns nefarious at the same level at which it can be furthered by good omens.

That I left the commune of via Andrea Fulvio with a bitter taste in my mouth.

Perhaps I should have given time the time to sweeten it.

At this point I no longer understand anything, I no longer know. I know I'm on a train to Brindisi - that the rest belongs to afterwards, to the bright and black tomorrows. That I write, that I have written.

*

29/1/1971 Rome
That green grass, shady and fresh. That the great sea of great relaxedness appears. That Rome, the athletic breeze of February 1970, that the breeze of 6th February 1970, opportunistically and indifferently covers my truths with its sand. Who knows! After how much coagulated blood I shall fall into the destructo-creative machine of the universe.

That today I am happy to be what I am, to rest my feet on the marble of Trinità dei Monti, to smoke a filterless gauloises. That I am the sky blue of a watercolour palette. That the diamond gong thriceshivers intermittently a rhythmically rhytmical sound. That throbbing tattoo. That the warm wave travels warmly. That the warm wave penetrates all matter. That I seek silence. That I seek silence filled with sweet perfumes. That the neuropathic, neuroparanoid silence

That I am happy. That I am happy rejoicing in the void, the empty void. The empty void that encloses nothing, not even happiness. That still the illusory, delicate beneficial friend, true lover, humanely godly god, dogma believed in from the depths of the heart. That it slips into the blood like a good thief. That the candle weeps the last tears of its body. That I scream out my joy at being. That I scream out my joy at being able to scream out my doubtful serenity. That I feel the flash of love, peace, serenity, trust, of living without thinking. That I god. That I great god. That I greatest god. That I believed-in dogma. That the waves vibrate. That the vibrational waves bounce back.. That the marks drawn on this sheet leave the vibrational waves. That these marks are part of my situational dimension.That blagging. That blagging is part of my situational dimension. That in the middle of my chest I feel forces pushing against my ribcage. That I feel forces at war. That I feel a great force. Force raging for an outlet. Force at war. Force that would create. Force that already has created.

*

I was 14 when the flesh of my being turned into warm bone. I was 14 when the flesh of my worm turned into warm bone. And it curved like the muzzle of a trotting horse over the curls of two lips suckling the seed of life. Three crosses and a beardless friar, on the earth that drinks the blood of God/Love for the situation that was born/That the vibrating waves rend the darkness and the thick nebulous density of my truths. And the great refusal of the scarlet shroud of death. That I am weeping over a notebook found in the Pincio caves. Green grass shady and fresh. That the great sea of relaxedness. That Rome. That the big raindrops and atlantic breeze of March 6, 1970. That from those with their own wave to the great sounds that the breeze of March 6, 1970 is covering in the sand of opportunistically situational indifference, the massacres, the carnage of my truths. After how much coagulated blood shall I mass up my creed in the destructo-creative machine of space.

*

O dearest.
O masterful death.
O supremely serene death.
O invoked death.
O fearsome death.
O indecipherable death.
O strange death.
O long live death.
O death which is death.
Death that puts a stop to this vibrating lightning bolt.

Sarah Lawson and Malgorzata Koraszewska
Six poems from Anna Kühn-Cichocka's
A Little Town With a View on the River

ANNA KÜHN-CICHOCKA (b. 1940 in Wloclawek) holds a degree in sociology and has taught at various levels, from primary school to Polish classes in secondary school. She is an artist, painting mainly in oils, and also a poet with a keen eye for visual details. She now lives in Plock, another town on the Vistula River northwest of Warsaw. Although she had never visited the small town of Dobrzyn nad Wisla (which lies between Wloclawek and Plock), a friend of hers who had grown up there told her so much about the town that she decided to write about it herself, imagining herself into the 'feel' of the town and its characters. In 2003 she published a poetry pamphlet called *A Little Town with a View on the River (Miasteczko z widokiem na rzeke)* with her imaginative re-creation of life in Dobrzyn nad Wisla. To her surprise and gratification, people from all parts of Poland have written to her to say that she has described their own small town to a T! These poems are a selection from that series of evocative snapshots.

here the houses
grazed quietly
under the watchful eye
of the church tower
it was high
made of brick
with a six-sided
sharply pointed roof
it seemed to be
a huge pencil
to write down
our misdemeanours
on blue pages of the sky

the organist played beautifully
but his singing was worse
sometimes from a nearby meadow
sheep answered him

at Christmas time
women with their whole heart and throat
tore Christmas carols to shreds
the plaster baby
stopped his ears with his little fists
but God smiled under his moustache
and gave absolution

*

on rainy days
we discovered
a wonderful world of attics
here lived
a clock with a late cuckoo
remembering better times
the old trunk
full of mysteries
wrapped in torn lace
an iron that had run out of steam
and lost its shirt
countless objects
which had already forgotten
who needed them
and for what

we sat in rickety armchairs
the dust danced in the light of a candle
sometimes a floorboard creaked
or a spring moaned
spiders spun
stories about ghosts
and fear
had bigger and bigger eyes

*

beyond the river
the sky was high
and somebody
cut all the shades of green
into rectangles
and shuffled them
on the bank
the trees whispered about something
other trees
singly and in groups
were going off beyond the horizon

the silence ripened
in the scorching heat of noon

houses
sleepily squinted their shutters
wasps fell into doughnuts
through the open shop doors
we drank lemonade pink and warm
sharing fairly
sips tasting of acid drops

in sweaty hands
we clasped the Summer

*

the doctor knew everybody from birth
he ran quickly through the little streets
and his white hair and coat
blew in the wind
he was sharp tongued
had golden hands
and a wife like a syringe
even old men were afraid
of the doctor's wife
she was lean and noisy
she shouted at many of them
that they couldn't even make a baby
when they were sober
and that they stinted on soap
but when disaster struck
she was the first to help
that's why
they made deep bows to her
from a distance
and escaped to the other side of the street

*

the inn was at the market place
re-christened Freedom Square
after the War
Saturday's guests grew ripe
on the scanty lawn
and gap-toothed benches

a thin mongrel on the steps
waited for a benevolent bone

towards morning
from the open door flowed
thick cigarette smoke
richly ornamented with the aroma
of beer sausages vodka and herrings

the day got up with difficulty
Franek's missus was cleaning up
streams of soapy water
flowed on the pavement

the mongrel ravenously
devoured the gift

with a booming fist the church bell
hammered the drunken skulls
and it was Sunday already

*

the barmaid Halinka
was known to everybody in town
she was a robust woman
some 15 stone by the look of her
and one or another
of the more drunken customers
would want to marry her
at once
both Summer and Winter
she wore tight blouses
with the neckline cut
all the way down to the brims of the glasses

Marilyn Hacker
Guy Goffette's 'Construction Site of the Elegy'

GUY GOFFETTE is one of the most unabashedly lyrical contemporary French poets, a man from northern France (born in the Ardennes in 1946) who claims Verlaine, issued from the same geography, as one of his literary godfathers with no compunction. Goffette makes frequent homage to his sources, however oblique, in an ongoing series of 'Dilectures' - doubled readings/readings of predilection and delectation: deft verse portraits of writers as diverse as Auden, Ritsos, Borges, Max Jacob, Valéry Larbaud, Pound, Pavese, Rimbaud, and, of course, Verlaine, to whom he also devoted a prose book, neither biography nor criticism but a poet's re-imagination of another poet's life and mind. He has written a similar volume on Bonnard (some of his verse homages are to visual artists as well). Auden, that least French of poets, has fascinated Guy Goffette for years, and his latest, just-published book, *L'Oeil de la baleine*, confronts him in a similarly idiosyncratic prose encounter.

Despite these homages and acknowledgements of origins, Goffette's is not at all a 'literary', referential, even less a self-referential poetry. Rather, he is a poet who makes use (as Paul Claudel stated in his own *ars poetica*) of quotidian words, everyday expressions, and makes them new, re-invests them with humour, connotation and emotion, and with a tragi-comic festivity. He is also a poet whose work, in subtext, dialogues with the past of French poetry itself, though this dialogue is an undercurrent, never diverting the poem from its primary direction. The witty 'Charlestown Blues',* for example, written during a residence in Rimbaud's Charleville, makes use of the decasyllabic dixain, which a French reader would first associate, not with the Verlaine/Rimbaud duo/duel but with Maurice Scève's mysterious 'Délie', published in Lyon in 1544.

As part of this dialogue, Guy Goffette's ludic tug-of-war with the sonnet, which is evident in his three most recent books, is one thing that drew me to his work, as a poet who, myself, have often handled, de- and re-constructed the form. Goffette has written wry, contemporary rhymed sonnets in alexandrines. But a thirteen-line poem, as part of a sequence or standing on its own, made up of three usually unrhymed quatrains and a last line which sometimes, though not always, mounts to the classic 12 syllables, has become Goffette's 'signature' strophe since his 1991 collection *La Vie promise*, and he has continued to use it in his two subsequent books.

'The Construction Site of the Elegy' ('le Chantier de l'Elégie'), while not a sonnet sequence, reveals Goffette's techniques and preoccupation: for example, the juxtaposition of a quotidian situation and a philosophical preoccupation; the site of the pastoral made contemporary in its details; the use of prolonged metaphor and simile, which - the musician, the 'Bateau Ivre' children - move to the forefront of the poem like contrapuntal protagonists; the themes of eros and thanatos, or rather, the erotic shadowed by the awareness of death; the ludic syntax, here manifest in a parenthetical statement which straddles sections two through five.

Guy Goffette lived in northern France for many years, and worked as a bookseller and as a schoolteacher. His austere and prematurely ruptured childhood is eloquently invoked in a book of prose memoirs, *Partance et autres lieux*, published in 2000. He has travelled widely, both near - Belgium and the Netherlands - and far, to Eastern Europe and to Louisiana, on the trail of the blues. Like his friend and mentor, the poet Jacques Réda, he is a jazz enthusiast. He now lives in central Paris, where he works as an editor at Gallimard, and is closely but informally allied with poet-friends of his own generation such as Hédi Kaddour and Paul de Roux, with whose work he also readily dialogues in the context of poems.

After a period in which much of French poetry eschewed the concrete, the narrative and the quotidian, Guy Goffette's poems have found an enthusiastic readership in the last two decades. He received the Grand Prix de Poésie of the Société des gens de lettres in 2000 for the entirety of his work. His early book, *Éloge pour une cuisine de province*, along with *La vie promise,* were re-issued in Gallimard's pocket-format Poésie series in 2000, and his latest collection, *Un manteau de fortune*, was awarded the Grand Prix de Poésie of the Académie française for 2001.

* Several of these can be read in translation in the Faber anthology *20th-Century French Poems*, edited by Stephen Romer.

Construction Site of the Elegy

I

Mowing the October lawn - the last
before the russet horde and the grip of winter,

despair (or what else if tomorrow
doesn't exist?) grips your throat

and it's not too much to say that one holds back tears
while stirring the green flour.

The machine beside you sputters bravely
as if it too were intoxicated

by this flow of bucolic blood
while on the threshold, the muse in an apron,

cutting short your dark reflections,
joins in, shouting 'Watch out

for your shirt, grass stains!' (In the end,
despair's not so bad, it's even

a kind of consolation, the evening's
pill which drops without a splash

into the elixir of old lovers.)

II

(And to think that for us, spring
was married beneath the flowering hawthorn,

that everything was decked out for a one-way
trip to the heart of the grove:

the red roofs, the blued spine
of the hills, and the trees already

crossing their arms against the sky
as if nothing ever again

would change, despite the rain,
the wind, the hail, and the distress

shared by the musician who in the midst
of an opera doubts that he likes music

and still must hear it, must put up with it
and who remains seated nonetheless

among the elegy's accessories
like those statues at the far end of the park

knitting silence for the exhausted gods.

III

And to think that we believed in happiness
like kids flying their boat's flag

over a stagnant puddle in the alley
- they know that a breath would be enough

to spill the sea across its keel
but make believe while waiting

for a bigger wounding wave
to take away their taste for being

on first-name terms with eternity. We too,
we believed that the earth turned

in our arms, and would always turn
like the sun orbiting the apple-tree

a peaceful torpor, when the worm
was already beneath the bark

the tools sharpened in the burning shed
and blood boiling in the muscles

of the dream-butchers.

IV

But death has passed its heavy hand
through the thick hair of summers

and the last sun has made a torch
before us from the rags of the lime-tree

splashing with purple and gold as usual
the closed garden of our love

and our eyes, then the fog
came, and your tears, and winter

snagging on the horizon's barbed wire
the first ball-gown, the seamless

dress and the unkept promise
to change the water of our days to wine

to change the water, every day,
and thirst, and the sea,

the world's bitter face,
every day

- in vain.

V

This is how, evening after evening,
we became mortal

blaming fatigue, cold,
and the distance of bodies suddenly

exhausted into heaviness, as if
the apple in its roundness held

in our pale hands, escaping them
had scattered on the earth

what was left in us of the old paradise.
This is how, night after night

we've become alone
like the mirrors in children's bedrooms

in a foreclosed house: open
on the fading angel wallpaper

and henceforth with no other future
but demolition, stone by stone

of what was also the canopy
above our bed, the story endlessly

repeated of love o flaccid
hostage of time and boredom)

VI

Even if executioner and victim now
are merged or erased, the job

is done, and the grass brought to the dump
praised to the skies by crows,

and we can henceforth go from the executioner's
dollar-green block to the creamy basket of bedrooms

without washing our eyes since a head
has already rolled somewhere

spilling its tumbril of tears
close to the apple tree carding the horizon:

the body is taken which thought to take
and hold the one love in its arms

where all, all is loss, and finished
by collapsing like a wall or like

that old thistle-spike which blunted the scythe.

Belinda Cooke and Richard McKane
Six Poems by Boris Poplavsky

BORIS POPLAVSKY was born in Moscow on May 24th 1903. After the 1917 Revolution he and his father moved to Yalta where his writing career was to begin. In 1919 he emigrated to Constantinople before finally settling in Paris in 1921 where he remained until his life was cut short in October 1935. His death was the result of a tragic accident. One night Poplavsky, who was quite heavily involved in drugs, met up with a fellow addict who was planning to take his own life. Unfortunately he managed to include Poplavsky in his plans. Poplavsky's death resulted from an overdose of narcotics mixed with poison. He was first introduced to drugs at the age of twelve by his sister (a cocaine addict), and regularly used hard drugs throughout his life. Living life on the edge in this way meant he was always at risk of meeting such a death.

At the time of his death Poplavsky had only published one book of poems, *Flags* (1930). However, by this time he had already built up quite a reputation. His posthumous collections include: *Snowy Hour* (1936), *From a Garland of Wax* (1938) and *Airship of an Unknown Direction* (1965). He also completed one novel, *Apollo Unformed*, and started another, *Home from the Heavens*, as well as writing extensive journals.

Poplavsky belongs to the younger generation of those who left Russia after the Revolution. Akhmatova, in 'Poem without a Hero', says of the Russian émigré: 'the air of exile is bitter like poisoned wine', but for the younger poets it was particularly difficult. They had less access to émigré journals which were edited predominantly by poets who had established themselves before leaving Russia. They had also a more limited experience of the culture they had left behind. Poplavsky, in his poem 'Departure from Yalta', does suggest nostalgia for Russia but in much of his poetry one feels that his is more concerned with expressing his feelings about life in bohemian Paris where he describes himself at one with its many outsiders.

Poplavsky's poetry shows the influence of French poetry, in particular avant-garde movements such as French Surrealism. Indeed, if he had lived, it is likely he would have written increasingly in the French language. Poplavsky's poetry can be difficult at times and is best read as a whole, for this allows one to note the cumulative effect of certain images that run through his poems: angels, roses, flags, the Titanic, to name just a few. At its best though, Poplavsky's poetry is extremely poignant. He comes across as a Hamlet-like figure troubled by the experience of remaining alive in the world. He is also concerned with a wide range of religious beliefs but ends up once more with a Christian God though his relationship with him is somewhat ambivalent.

Poplavsky enjoys wordplay in his poems and this, not surprisingly, is impossible to convey in translation. However, the novelty with which he personifies nature (possibly under the influence of Pasternak), his moving direct statements, and the fluidity of many of his images, all provide many satisfying opportunities for the would-be translator. All in all, Poplavsky, as the outsider, managed to find in his adopted country a context for moving poetry: exile becomes the subject matter that makes his poetry powerful.

Departure from Yalta

It rained all night. The storm had already lasted a month.
At the entrance to the damp forest the wicket gate was
banging on its wrecked hinges. Dark and circling,
the river of the skies rushed off to the south.

The river was as busy as a highway.
The hoarding rattled above the damp pavilion.
The passer-by, head well down, turned
into the alley, where all is still green.

Over the tall jetty the white mist flew up
circling, and then dropped back into the ocean.
There above the rocks the tower's black globe
gives advance warning of the hurricane.

Screaming out over carrion the jackdaws arrive;
their battle with the weather foreshadows the winter.
The wave in flight from the pebbled shore
flings itself dust-laden onto the shop windows.

Everything has been locked up, the benches emptied.
Only the newspaper seller sends out his piercing cry.
High up in the cold the chimneys talk their usual nonsense,
and a distant shot rings out from the mountains.

Everything is asleep. Dawn is not far away.
So drink, dear friend, let's smash our glasses.
Let's wind up this fine old gramophone
and carelessly sing along together.

We understood, we defeated evil,
we did everything that glitters in the cold.
We rejected everything, snow blocked our path,
so drink my friend, let's smash our glasses.

And as for Russia we shall not weep for her!
Candles will go out on Christmas trees, and we shall sleep.
The candles will die and it will be dark over the trees,
and they will burn with stars and eternity.

Throughout that night the soldiers sang till dawn,
until finally they grew cold, silent and downcast.
With nothing left to drink they could only wait for day....
its sullen face appears and the wind blows interminably.

Now is not the time to waste your strength!
There in a deep sleep the secret homeland dawns.
Though it is winter without us, the years like white snow,
the snowdrifts grow and grow in order one day to melt.

And only you can tell the young
of that about which they sang and wept till dawn,
and only you will sing about pity for the fallen,
about eternal love expecting no reply.

For the last time the priest on the mountain
served the mass. Morning rose
and in the small neighbouring monastery
one more sick soul departed into eternity.

The hull of the ship shines, immense and severe:
who is this solitary watcher hands thrust in overcoat?
How slowly it turns red in the night time east!
Who can believe there are so many years of parting...

Who could have known then... that it was that or death?
Peacefully the old man raised the Eucharist...
that we might believe, weep and burn with longing,
but never speak of happiness.

Eagles

I remember the varnished wings of the carriage,
silence and lies. Fly sunset, fly.
This is how Christopher Columbus hid from the crew
the immensity of the voyage they had made.

The crooked back of the coachman
was encircled with orange glory.
Grey hair curled under the hard hat,
and in the back us, like a two-headed eagle.

I look, my eyes avoiding the sun,
which still manages to dazzle even more...
the powdered implacable beak
threatens passers-by till they blink and shiver.

You threatened me for eighteen days,
on the nineteenth you softened and faded.
The sunset finally left off playing on the panes:
suddenly it turned noticeably colder.

Autumn smoke rose over the carriage
where our happiness was slow to depart,
but the captain kept from the crew
the immensity of the voyage they had made.

1923

Prayer

The night is weary. And the moon goes in.
Somewhere a morning train whistles past.
It's terrible to think how time passes,
you can neither think nor live.

you ≠ one !

Endlessly we try to forget, to sink
into oblivion, walking, joking or dealing cards.
Why not present yourself for the Day of Judgment?
Rid yourself of fear through emptiness?

Or coming down from drugs
to see the pale and terrible night -
like dying from a restaurant window,
and no one any longer has the strength to help.

No, beneath the moon's glow
I will remember fate in the field,
and listen to the far-off barking in the mist,
and grieve for the evil that has been done.

my l ?
I've ?

Better for me to open my heart to
the scepticism, the meaningless dark,
to condemn and humble myself,
and turn defencelessly towards Him.

Romance

IMp. 11

The emerald sky shines,
the town is dark, the square mysterious,
Salome - the soul forgets,
how your voice was like death.

And now I remember, you came out of the sunset,
a black cup in your slender hands. To the song
of the white acacia, the evening moved away...
beyond the river and into the clouds.

Everything seemed pointless and strange.
The black knight shut his eyes. The restaurant
orchestra swam over the marsh,
and into the interminable distance.

Sleeping spectre, there is no way
I can wake you, I am your dream.
Bending low, Salome sang
over the marsh waters in harmony.

Time will fly past, yesterday's black-winged
spectre of the earth will disappear.
I shall wait for you in the castle tower,
where the star hums in the distance.

Golden, unique and alive
inseparable from you throughout the ages.
Sleep my knight, above Roncevaux,
how wonderful are those fires in the clouds.

So that you will not see sadness
and will live happily through this year,
I shall throw the black cup into the sea;
I shall walk off into the radiance of the marshes.

The years turn pink on the mountains.
All that is past is close to spring.
There under the bright star of freedom
memory sleeps, smiling in its dreams.

Seraphita I

The call of electric violins was born in the darkness,
the ship was sinking to the bottom on the huge screen,
the rain made a rain noise on the asphalt. Roulette was rattling in a hut.
On the threshold of freedom do you remember this spring?

You closed your eyes and went off into the terrible distance,
Tannhäuser in vain shouted about death on the gramophone.
You were far away, perhaps you had ascended to heaven,
the world shone before you like the morning snow and was silent.

Constellations burst and worlds were born in roses,
but I fell by an invisible door during the singing of life.
O Mary, there in the abyss mention my name,
perhaps I'll hear, perhaps I'll remember that shore.

Your dream was so deep that the gilded thread
could break unnoticed. Now you seem not to breathe.
I begged you to come down from the bustle of life.
I begged and hoped that perhaps you won't hear.

Only a voice was born. Oh, I didn't understand at first,
it was born in such exhaustion, flew for so long
just like a bird that eternity rocked on wings over the sea.
It was surprised with itself and wanted to listen to itself.

'I am with you forever. I will not lose you in heaven.
I carried away this dark name into the circles of dawn and sunset.
I go to sleep, get lost, get weak, fly, die.
The angel with the white name is with me over the chaos of evil.'

Only light, just like a yellow blade, came out of the dark.
The performance was over. Rainy spring faded.
Time passes quickly, but the heart knows no terror.
The heart hears the praying of names in the circle of the dawn.

*

The whole day in a cold, dirty shroud
the dreamer slept, forgetting the world.
In the morning there was a swimming contest,
the trumpets played on the tug.

Sweaty rowers shouted from the rowing boats,
the people clapped loudly on the bridges.
In a gust of wind to freedom
the flags tore off the windows and poles.

The wind blew the newspapers onto the water,
dust flew from the boulevard into the blue.
By the station a balloon twisted
in the branches of a lime-tree bare of leaves.

All those who hadn't gone away for summer
shuffled the yellow leaves on the boulevard
and squinting at the sky made out
the announcement on the air balloon.

They were all cheerful, smiled
and did not let each other be sad,
as though they had never been wrong,
as though they had expected nothing.

Tired of the motley, lazy day
they returned home exhausted
in the hour when in a sick paralysis
the dreamer got up and opened the window.

Cecilia Rossi
Poems from Alejandra Pizarnik's *Works and Nights*

BORN in 1936 in the town of Avellaneda, a Southern suburb of the city of Buenos Aires, Pizarnik was the second daughter of Russian Jewish immigrants. In her short life - Pizarnik died in September 1972 - she was to produce one of the most compelling poetic works in the Argentine canon. Her friend, linguist and poet Ivonne Bordelois recalls the occasion when she accompanied Pizarnik to Jorge Luis Borges's house in order to interview him for the literary magazine *Zona Franca*. The questions had been planned by Pizarnik, who, nevertheless, remained for most of the visit 'curled up like a hypnotised cat in an armchair in Borges's house' while Bordelois conducted the interview. She recalls how she felt at the time, 'moving between these two Himalayas of our literature, so opposed between them and, at the same time, both of them writers that only Argentina could produce, with such a special amalgam of European and porteño roots...' Pizarnik's favourite Borges poem, which she regarded as one of his best poems, 'Mateo, XXV, 30', found its way into one of her last poems (dated 1971), as part of the typical 'intertextual fusions' she used to practise:

- We gave you all that was necessary for you to understand
and you preferred the wait,
as if all announced to you the poem
(the one you'll never write because it is an inaccessible garden

- I only came to see the garden -)

-Te dimos todo lo necesario para que comprendieras
y preferiste la espera,
como si todo te anunciase el poema
(aquel que nunca escribirás porque es un jardín inaccesible

- solo vine a ver el jardín -)

Another great Argentine writer, Julio Cortázar, who also became a close friend of Pizarnik's when they met in Paris in 1960, dedicated a poem to her, entitled 'Aquí Alejandra' which shows the warm regard and esteem he felt for the young poet. Their friendship is also evidenced in his many letters to Pizarnik, compiled in his *Cartas* (edited by Aurora Bernárdez and published in 2000). In his poem Alejandra is his *bicho* and so he pleads with her to:

curl up here, drink with me,
look, I have called them,

they will surely come, the intermediaries,
the party for you, the whole party...

acurrúcate aquí, bebé conmigo,
mirá, las he llamado,
vendrán seguro las intercesoras,
el party para vos, la fiesta entera...

The above references to two major figures of the Argentine literary canon in connection with Pizarnik offer an insight into her position within that same canon. When years later she achieved the status of major poet, such status was by no means the result of her untimely death. Early in her literary career, living in Paris with a number of Latin American writers, she met Octavio Paz, who acknowledged her great talent and unusual poetic gift. In his prologue to Pizarnik's fourth collection *Árbol de Diana* (1962) he described the volume as 'an object (animate) which allows us to see beyond, a natural instrument of vision'. This statement, for the young Pizarnik brought up reading French poets, such as Rimbaud and Mallarmé, signified a major breakthrough. Her poetic fate had been sealed: she would devote her life to poetry - to poetry understood as a 'space of revelations', as a place in which to live herself - and set out to write a poetry that would construct her identity as poet, making the body of the poem with her body... 'No quiero ir/nada más/que hasta el fondo' (I don't want to go/ anywhere/ but to the end) was found among other texts written on the chalkboard in her workroom after she died. The poems in *Works and Nights* (1965) are evidence of this process and mark Pizarnik's mature poetic voice. The key question for the translator is how to translate this construction of subjectivity, this subject-in-process, to borrow Julia Kristeva's term, which is indeed a question Pizarnik herself addressed in her sixth collection, *Extracción de la piedra de locura (The Cure of Folly)* (1968): '¿Qué significa traducirse en palabras?/ What does it mean to translate oneself into words?'

Revelations

Beside you in the night
words are clues, keys.
A king, the desire to die.

That your body always be
a beloved space of revelations.

He who illumines

When you look at me
my eyes are keys,
the wall has secrets,
my fear words, poems.
Only you make of my memory
a fascinated traveller,
an incessant fire.

Acknowledgement

You make the silence of lilacs which shake
in my tragedy of the wind in my heart.
You made of my life a children's story
where shipwrecks and deaths
are excuses for adorable ceremonies.

Presence

your voice
in this being unable to move away
from my gaze
things dispossess me
make of me a ship on a river of stones
if your voice is not
rain alone in my feverish silence
you unbind my eyes
and please
may you never stop
speaking
ever

Encounter

Someone enters the silence and abandons me.
Now solitude is not alone.
You speak like the night.
Announce yourself like thirst.

Duration

He departed in the black night
and his body was to dwell in this room
where my sobs, dangerous footsteps
of who will not come, yet here is his presence
moored to this bed where my sobs
because a face calls,
set in the dark,
precious stone.

Your voice

Ambushed in my writing
you sing in my poem.
Hostage to your sweet voice
petrified in my memory.
Bird given to flight.
Air tattooed by absence.
Clock that beats with me
so that I'll never wake.

The lost steps

Before it was a light
in my language born
a few steps from love.

Open night. Night of presence.

Encircled by avidity

When it does come my eyes will shine
with the light of whom I weep
but now it kindles a rumour of flight
in the heart of every thing.

To name you

Not the poem of your absence,
only a drawing, a crack on a wall,
something in the wind, a bitter taste.

Works and nights

to make of thirst my emblem
to mean the only dream
not to nourish on love ever again

I have been pure offering
pure roaming
of wolf in woods
in the night of bodies

to speak the innocent word

Sense of absence

if I dare
look up and speak
it is because of the shadow
so gently bound
to my name
far away
in the rain
in my memory
by a face
that burning in my poem
beautifully disperses
the scent
of the dear face gone

Childhood

An hour when grass grows
in the memory of a horse.
The wind delivers ingenuous speeches
in honour of lilacs,
and someone enters death
eyes wide open
like Alice in the country of what's been seen.

Daybreak

Naked dreaming a solar night.
I have lain for animal days.
The wind and the rain have erased me
as they would a fire, a poem
written on a wall.

In a place to escape oneself

Space. Long wait.
Nobody comes. This shadow.

To give it what all give it:
shady meanings,
not shaded.

Space. Burning silence.
What do shadows give one another?

Silences

Death always nearby.
I hear her say.
I only hear myself.

Party

I have displayed my orphanhood
on the table, like a map.
I have drawn the route
towards my place in the wind.
Those who arrive cannot find me.
Those I await do not exist.

And I have drunk furious liquors
to transmute faces
into an angel, into empty glasses.

Room alone

If you dare surprise
the truth about this old wall;
and its fissures, rents,
forming faces, sphinxes,
hands, clepsydras,
surely a presence
for your thirst will come,
no doubt this absence
that drinks you will go.

The truth about this old wall

that it's cold it's green that it moves too
calls gasps croaks it's halo hail
threads tremble shake
                              threads
it's green I'm dying
it's wall wall alone mute look it's dying

Invocations

Insist on your embrace,
double your fury,
create a space of slander
between the mirror and I
create a leper's song
between I and who I think I am.

Memory loss

Although the voice (his oblivion
overturning me as marooned as I am)
officiates in a petrified garden

I remember with all my lives
why it is I forget.

Forms

I don't know if bird or cage
murderous hand
or young woman dead among candles
or amazon panting in the great dark throat
or silent
yet perhaps loud like a fountain
perhaps minstrel
or princess in the highest tower

Memory
For Jorge Gaitán Durán

Harp of silence
where fear nests.
Moon moan of things
signifying absence.

Space of closed colour.
Someone hammers and builds
a coffin for time,
another coffin for light.

Shadow of the days to come
For Ivonne A. Bordelois

Tomorrow
they will dress me in ashes at dawn,
they will fill my mouth with flowers.
I will learn to sleep
in the memory of a wall,
in the breathing
of a dreaming animal.

Twilight

The shadow covers familiar petals
The wind robs the last nod of a leaf
The sea alien and doubly mute
in the summer whose lights move us to pity

A desire from here
A memory from there

Dwellings

For Théodore Fraenkel

In the clawing hand of a dead man,
in the memory of a madman,
in the sadness of a child,
in the hand searching for a glass,
in the unreachable glass,
in the usual thirst.

Beggar voice

And yet I dare to love
the sound of light at a dead hour,
the colour of time on an abandoned wall.

In my gaze I have lost it all.
So far to ask. So near to know there is not.

Terence Cave
A memorial note on Edith McMorran
and a translation of Aragon's 'C'

THIS translation was presented as part of a collective tribute offered on 23 October 2004 at St Hugh's College, Oxford, to the memory of Edith McMorran, who died on 1 December 2003. Edith McMorran was remembered not only as a loyal friend, colleague and tutor, but also as the founder and presiding spirit of the extraordinarily successful series of colloquia known as 'Translation in Oxford' (TRIO). She did most of the administration and the organisation, she often provided supplementary hospitality in her own home, and she made the programmes varied and interesting enough to attract speakers and audiences, not only from within the Modern Languages Faculty, but also from outside the University and indeed from a wider public.

Edith came from a French Jewish family; their family business, Frank et fils, was expropriated under the occupation of France in the Second World War and the family - together with Edith, who was of course at that time a small child - fled Paris just in time to avoid almost certain deportation.

The poem translated here comes from a collection of resistance poems written by Louis Aragon in 1942. The first, which is simply called 'C', is an indirect, understated, marginally surrealistic parody of false romantic fictions of the national past, shifting to a condensed evocation of the desolation of war. The opening line of the original ('J'ai traversé les ponts de Cé') refers to a real place in western France, just south of Angers, which marked the frontier of Caesar's invasion of Gaul ('Cé' is an abbreviation of 'César'). Aragon uses the reference in order to evoke the border between occupied France and the parts of the country not yet subject to the occupying authorities; 'Cé' is also the syllable that determines the rhyme of every line. I found it impossible to render this double device in English. I changed the title 'C' to 'S' to make the rhyme easier and invented a mythical 'Esse', a name which can be heard both as French (as in the noun ending '-esse') and as German and may thus suggest the treacherous blending of the occupier with the occupied.

At the memorial event, I read the translation and played a recording of a setting of the original poem by Francis Poulenc, a composer whom Edith herself much admired. The setting brings out the latent warmth as well as the irony of the poem.

C

J'ai traversé les ponts de Cé
C'est là que tout a commencé

Une chanson des temps passés
Parle d'un chevalier blessé

D'une rose sur la chaussée
Et d'un corsage délacé

Du château d'un duc insensé
Et des cygnes dans les fossés

De la prairie où vient danser
Une éternelle fiancée

Et j'ai bu comme un lait glacé
Le long lai des gloires faussées

La Loire emporte mes pensées
Aves les voitures versées

Et les armes désamorcées
Et les larmes mal effacées

Ô ma France ô ma délaissée
J'ai traversé les ponts de Cé

S

I crossed the bridges into Esse
That's where it all began alas

An ancient lay from Lyonesse
Tells of a wounded knight's distress

Of a rose trampled in the press
Of a fine lady's unlaced dress

Of a mad duke in his fortress
With moat and swans keen to impress

Of an always betrothed princess
Dancing across the sunlit grass

And I saw like snow lying on glass
The endless lie of glories past

The Loire flows on thoughts leave no trace
Past trucks gutted and driverless

Weapons made safe under duress
And tears undried on every face

O France betrayed without redress
I crossed the bridges into Esse

Paul Batchelor
Morphic Cubism: The Strange Case of Gwillam Mad MacSweeney
(Barry MacSweeney, *Horses in Boiling Blood*, Equipage, 2005)

Feedback

IN A winning but eccentric overestimation, Tristan Tzara praised Apollinaire for his use of 'the exact, real, totally unpromiscuous nudity of the word which is only itself, intended in its round force, with no background of allusions, or, rather, with none of the seductions of sublimated imagery'. It is a moot point whether a language that achieved such an ideal would prove perfectly suitable to translation or impossible to carry over. In either case it is truer to say that Apollinaire's practice was centred on linguistic phenomena particularly subject to their cultural moment. Humour, obscure literary allusion (often an echo in the cadence of a line), deliberate tonal misfires and à la mode cultural references depend on nuances of language and an intimacy with one's audience. Consider the opening line of 'Zone', the first poem in *Alcools*: 'A la fin tu es las de ce monde ancien.' The tone is colloquial, but the line is a traditional alexandrine. The reader is addressed familiarly, but 'ancien' is required to take up the traditional three syllables, instead of eliding into two, as it would in conversational speech. Cadence and meaning are held in a useful torsion. Such incongruities, essential to Apollinaire's poetry, are lost in the literal translation: 'Finally you are tired of the ancient world.'

There are few literal translations in *Horses in Boiling Blood*. While MacSweeney finds some ingenious linguistic equivalents ('Listen Its Plutting', lovingly makes use of a Northumbrian dialect word for rain of French origin), his typical mode is somewhat more unbuttoned. In 'Les Fenêtres' Apollinaire writes 'Les Chabins chantent des airs à mourir/Aux Chabines marronnes.' These lines contain considerable wordplay: 'Chabins' and 'Chabines' were terms used in the Antilles to describe the offspring of mixed marriages between Negroes and mulattos. 'Chabins' is also a phonetic pun on 'le chabanais' ('noise' or 'racket'). The phrase 'des airs à mourir' contains several possible meanings (the Chabins may sing 'killing songs' or may 'sing one to death'), and sounds close to 'mourir d'amour' (to be 'dying of love', with sexual overtones). A literal translation would read 'The rams sing sad songs/To the brown ewes.' MacSweeney's 'The Garden Door is Open On The World' translates these lines as 'The big rammes at Hexham are doing what they do best ramming/So the ewes have gone berserk up on the top fields aching to be tupped.' Here, 'tupped' evokes some of Apollinaire's wordplay, as it recalls Iago waking Brabantio with the cry 'an old black ram/Is tupping your white ewe.' The Chattertonesque kenning 'rammes' is one of the many references to Chatterton that recur throughout *Horses in Boiling Blood*. In this case, it may refer to 'The Battle of Hastynges', which includes the lines: 'As when two bulles, destynde for Hochtide fyghte/ Are yoked by the necke within a sparr.' Clive Bush has noted that MacSweeney adapted this image in *Brother Wolf* (his homage to Chatterton), describing a farming practice at Sparty Lea:

up there they
strap two
rams together the
hardest-headed
wins. Death
on the horns.

Such a network of buried allusion is indicative of the privacy of MacSweeney's endeavour: for all the theatricality, we are never far from the lonely room of the exile/autodidact. What interests me here is how this 'privacy' impacts on our reading experience. When we read, say, Lowell's *Imitations* there is always a putative original to be consulted. To experience the imitation as imitation, the reader is required to have some knowledge of the original author/poem/context, as well as a familiarity with Lowell himself: cross-referencing is expected. In contrast, MacSweeney does not appear as a distinct personality in his versions; it is as if the process of translation began at a much earlier stage. Perhaps this is to be expected: Apollinaire's example (his poetry, his life, his self-mythologising) proved crucial to MacSweeney's conception of what a poet should be. We might expect a certain amount of 'feedback', as techniques MacSweeney originally learned from Apollinaire are put to service in translations of Apollinaire himself.

Consider these lines from 'Souvenirs': 'Un monsieur en bras de chemise/ Se rase près de la fenêtre' ('A man in shirt sleeves/is shaving at the window'). MacSweeney's version ('Memories are Made of This') is as follows:

I was a man in a new-look baggy nightshirt starched and white
Trepanned because of a starreburst in the trenchant trenches
I stood by the window and shaved and shaved away my grievous unrest...

Later, I will consider MacSweeney's interpolated references to Apollinaire's biography. I want to draw attention to the way Apollinaire at his most plainspoken (Tzara would say 'unpromiscuous') has become distinctly MacSweeneyesque by the use of two of MacSweeney's linguistic hallmarks. First, MacSweeney's habit of placing the adjectives at the end of the line ('a new-look baggy nightshirt starched and white') creates a rhetorically inflated, orotund effect; the solemn tone enhances the comedy of the image. Second, MacSweeney's use of repetition ('I stood by the window and shaved and shaved') sounds in this instance rather Chaplinesque in its increasingly fevered attempts to accomplish a simple task. What is remarkable is the way MacSweeney's amplifications reinstate what is lost in literal translation: Apollinaire's beloved clash of registers.

Interpretative Imagery

Apollinaire used images as part of his effort to get beyond conceptual language, an approach influenced by the emerging Cubist movement. It follows that there is often a deliberate incongruity between the terms of comparison. For example, 'Fête' conflates images of shells, fireworks and breasts. As if slightly out of focus, these images never quite cohere, and the suppression of explanatory linking information, often present in Apollinaire's manuscripts but omitted from the published poems, heightens the suggestive uncertainty of tone. We come to see such discontinuity as a defining feature of Apollinaire's poetry. Consider these lines:

Il songe aux roses de Saadi
Et soudain sa tête se penche
Car une rose lui redit
La molle courbe d'une hanche

(He dreams of the roses of Saadi
And suddenly his head sinks down
As a rose evokes for him once more
The soft curve of a hip)

MacSweeney's rendering, in 'War Roses', is as follows:

The roses - my men - bleed like subjects from the rimdom
of the Marquis de Sade - and suddenly his head bends over -
a beautiful red rose reduced and reduced by Bosche brutality
Spreadeagled like your bedroom-lit softly curved haunch-hips

Apollinaire's figure bows his head in remembrance of past love. In 'War Roses' the Persian poet Saadi becomes de Sade (Apollinaire wrote essays on de Sade, and a Sadean novel), and the correspondingly violent image refers to a head wound, presumably Apollinaire's own shrapnel wound. The image of a wounded body then recalls a spread-eagled body on a bed; this may seem grotesque, but the image itself ('bedroom-lit softly curved haunch-hips') is tender and erotic.

Apollinaire's habit of removing essential information tacitly invites an ungoverned reading. Inevitably, MacSweeney's equivalents are more grounded (the reader knows that reading Apollinaire occasioned the poems) and this is enhanced through MacSweeney's references to the trenches (placing Apollinaire) and by his framing many poems as addresses to an absent loved one (placing himself). In other words, for all their capacious gallimaufry, the translations are subject to formal attempts at having their meanings contained or directed. This is distinct from the conventional practice of glossing (silently introducing expository material) and recalls MacSweeney's earliest published poems, which, as John Wilkinson has noted, 'suffer from an itch to ensure the reader (in the first place the loved woman) receives the message, a message frequently duller than the image-complex would permit the less governed reading'. Wilkinson cites 'To Lynn at Work whose Surname I don't know', the opening poem from MacSweeney's first collection, *The Boy from the Green Cabaret Tells of His Mother*, a poem notably influenced by the French poets MacSweeney was reading at the time.

Relocation, Relocation, Relocation!

So far, I have looked at ways MacSweeney 'carries over' Apollinaire into English. But there is more at stake: *Horses in Boiling Blood* is touted as 'a collaboration, a celebration' rather than a translation. The reader is never certain whether the speaker is Apollinaire, MacSweeney, or an amalgam of the two: 'Gwillam Mad MacSweeney', as he is called in 'Miss the Mississippi and Thee'. This hybrid figure is characterised by his ability to move freely between Newcastle in the late 1990s and the trenches of the First World War. (In fact, Apollinaire was an artilleryman for most of the war, and only in the trenches a short time before receiving the head wound from a piece of shrapnel that led to his being trepanned. MacSweeney invariably presents Apollinaire as wounded, equating trepanation to his own 'broken head', ie. his alcoholism.) The hybrid also has foreknowledge of his own death, and the coming atrocities of World War Two, and is separated from the object of his love. The sense of loss is related to the war and, more mysteriously, to the head wound.

The genesis of 'Gwillam Mad MacSweeney' appears to be an over-identification between translator and subject. In 'War Roses' MacSweeney translates 'L'air est plein d'un terrible alcool/Filtré des étoiles mi-closes' (the air is full of terrible alcohol/filtered through the half-closed stars) as 'The air is crammed with completely mad spirits', suggesting the Demons of his earlier work. Another version of the same poem, 'At the Hoppings', is more explicit about the nature of the Demons: 'I breathe alcoholism into the air/Then the starres and argent sky swoon through my filters.' Identification is matched with a relocation of the poems from Paris to Newcastle: 'La vie est variable aussi bien que l'Euripe' ('Life is uncertain as the tides of Euripus') becomes 'The whole of life is strange like the tidalmark at Blayney Row/Just beyond Dunston Staithes and Stella…' Such wilfully inapposite equivalents enable MacSweeney to achieve wildly variant effects by staying otherwise faithful to the original.

'La petite auto' includes this description of a car breaking down at night:
Je n'oublierai jamais ce voyage nocturne où nul de nous ne dit un mot
Ô départ sombre où mouraient nos 3 phares…
…et 3 fois nous nous arrêtâmes pour changer un pneu qui avait éclaté

Et quand après avoir passé l'après-midi
Par Fontainebleau

Nous arrivâmes à Paris
Au moment où l'on affichait la mobilisation
(I shall not forget this nocturnal journey during which none of us spoke
O sombre departure when our three headlights broke…
…and three times we had to stop to change a burst tyre

And when that afternoon we had passed
Through Fontainebleau
We arrived in Paris
At the moment in which they were putting up mobilisation posters)

MacSweeney's rendering, in 'The Illegal 2CV', is as follows:

I'll never forget the time the car broke down completely lightless
We were on the old A1 and it was utterly distressing
It was before the war of the spirit between us Before catastrophe…

We went past Dragonville and Belmont and arrived in Newcastle
And saw we were going to have to go and try & slaughter Germans
We turned in Grainger Street and looked at each other lost for words

Observed detail mutates into a paranoid imperative - but then, seemingly innocuous features of the writing process have long held a capacity to threaten MacSweeney: *The Book of Demons* presents us with a particularly malevolent representation of the usually abstract notion of a poet's voice, grown independent of the poet and breaking out into the world, trying to tempt him to suicide. Similarly, where another poet might make a literary allusion, MacSweeney will often introduce the figure of a poet into the poem: throughout his poetry, Shelley, Jim Morrison and Anne Sexton visit MacSweeney. MacSweeney's references to the First World War suggest just such an embattled attempt at translating Apollinaire's empirical self into the poems. As the registers swing between bathetic translationese ('We were on the old A1 and it was utterly distressing') and high-flown lyricism ('It was before the war of the spirit between us'), the effect is of a volatile, shifting surface: the identification all translators hope for has become something more akin to demonic possession.

IN *The Truth of Poetry*, Michael Hamburger criticises Apollinaire for his 'inability to resist conventional rhetoric and lyricism of a kind not truly compatible with his equally genuine passion for modernity'. De Chirico celebrates this characteristic in *Ritratto premonitore di Guillaume Apollinaire*, depicting the poet as a marble bust wearing sunglasses. Apollinaire appears to have drawn strength from his contradictions. Abandoning Cubism for Orphism, he defined Orphic art by its refusal to rely on structures borrowed from the visual sphere: the artist does not *reveal* reality, he *creates* it. Even here, the impulse to seek out new forms and structures leads Apollinaire back to a more traditional, Romantic idea of the artist.

The supposed polarity of 'Order and Adventure' (a longstanding cliché of Apollinaire criticism) is misleading: Apollinaire's fidelity to the chaotic moment of composition meant that he insisted on both - simultaneously if possible. MacSweeney's translations are faithful to that spirit, and *Horses in Boiling Blood* makes a compelling case for radical, creative translation. Champion of so many -isms, Apollinaire would surely have given this process a new name. The title of this essay is one suggestion.

Reviews

Angela Livingstone *Poems from Chevengur. Transposition of fifty passages from Andrei Platonov's novel 'Chevengur'*
Gilliland Press, Clacton-on-Sea. (84 pp, £10 ISBN 0 9537867 5 7)

THIS is an extraordinary enterprise, a double transposition, from Russian to English, prose to verse. Angela Livingstone's method is to weld words and phrases from a selected passage from Platonov's great novel, *Chevengur*, into a short poem, together with paraphrases and additional words of her own, its metrical and stanzaic forms dictated by the material. At the end of the book, the underlying passages from Platonov's prose are given in both the original and in translation, with words used in the poems in bold type, providing for the fascinating business of comparison. There is also a broad outline of the narrative of *Chevengur* (the name of an imaginary town deep in the steppe, where soon after 1917 a group of impatient Bolsheviks are keen to establish communism without delay).

The novel, written between 1926 and 1928 or '29, was suppressed in Russia for 60 years. It shows, unflinchingly and beguilingly, the élan with which the exponents of the new faith devastate all before them to prepare the way for communism, including the shooting and mass burial of many of the townspeople. Platonov has found a way of writing about and articulating the experience of simple people whose world has been obliterated by revolution, civil war and class war. He began the novel as a tribute to 'our country's builders' (its first title), but as he wrote it, its pervading sense of communism as a mysterious force - expected at any moment but with no one knowing what it might be or feel like when it comes - transformed the work into a treatment of death and destruction, of the end of everything. At the same time a dream-like calm reigns, and surviving humans seem to have more in common with the elements, wind, rain, sun, than with each other.

In her introduction Angela Livingstone, who has co-translated two volumes of Platonov's fiction and other work (with both Robert and Elizabeth Chandler), explains what drew her to make these poems: the 'quiet, puzzling, cliché-resistant prose of *Chevengur*, which seems to contain, like a lining, a latent, undeclared poetic version of itself', as well as a writing style in which the significant goes 'unsignalled and without a supportive context, as though the genuine [has] to lie beyond, or beneath, any employment of deliberate technique'.

The whole sequence begins and ends with two narrative poems; in the first a fisherman submerges himself in a lake, and in the last the fisherman's Bolshevik son, one of the central figures of the novel, does the same thing years later. The first poem uses Platonov's words closely:

Now Mitya never believed in death.
He'd only wanted to take a look -
it might be far better than village life
on the shores of a lake, it might be a new

province lying beneath the sky
as though at the bottom of cool water.
'I'll just go and stay there a little while,'
he said.

This poem can be compared to the original:

Secretly he did not believe in death at all, but the main thing was he wanted to
have a look and see what was there: it might be much more interesting than liv-
ing in a village or on the shore of a lake; he saw death as another province which
was located under the sky as if at the bottom of cool water, and it drew him.

A poem titled 'Hunger' uses only a very few of Platonov's words from
Chevengur, a key phrase, 'dog-bitten horses', being taken from his novel
The Foundation Pit (Kotlovan) and much from a novel of the period by
Boris Pil'nyak, with Angela Livingstone herself providing structure: 'trav-
elling to look for food, for food, / for food' (across stanzas).
Many of the poems are fine lyrics in their own right:

At dawn these workers change shift.
Rain falls asleep in the soil.

Sun takes over. Wind
busily rises, dishevels
trees. Sets grass and bushes
muttering.

Rain, still weary,
climbs to its feet again,
woken by warmth, collects
its body into clouds.

Desolation is especially powerfully captured in one poem about a dis-
used smithy that condenses Platonov's detail:

Spiderweb and light thin spider-corpses
are sinking to the floor to disintegrate
in unrecognisable dust. Everywhere
particles lie scattered, shards of things
once cherished, once the darlings of their children,
Chipped-off scraps-perhaps of human people,
or beetles or the nameless gnats of the earth.

Overall, with its 'grey' tone and humble stylistic level, its loose but tangible narrative setting and its running symbols - wind, rain, water, worms, burdock, people on the move, sleep-this poem-cycle makes a moving incursion into Platonov's world of bewilderment, expectancy, abandonment and loss.

Antony Wood

Cliff Ashcroft *Dreaming of Still Water*
Salt (94pp £8.99 ISBN: 1 847711 129)

Eugenio Montejo *The Trees: Selected Poems 1967-2004*
translated by Peter Boyle
(Salt 184pp £10.99 ISBN 1 844710 335)

THE past might be another country but increasingly it is the favoured destination of many modern poets. Such explorations inevitably bring the world of poetry closer to that of translation, with their reliance on secondary source texts or the re-imagining of classic works, effecting a metamorphosis of their own. In Cliff Ashcroft's enthralling 1996 collection, *Faithless* - one of the best poetry debuts of recent years - Roman London prostitutes rubbed shoulders with early eastern Christians, English Civil War visionaries with Spanish Civil War veterans, all sprung from a variety of source material including New Testament verses, ancient epitaphs and modern historical studies. His new work, *Dreaming of Still Water*, continues these excavations, interweaving appearances from Christianity (Lazarus, Augustine), the mythological (Hylas, Antigone) and the historical (Pliny, Kaspar Hauser, the wild boy of Aveyron), piling up layers like a city street in which the past co-exists with the present, awaiting rediscovery: 'I was rummaging amongst the garbage,' as Ashcroft notes in 'Martyr's Scroll', 'for cloth or mosaic, looked-over valuables'.

As in *Faithless*, too, Ashcroft continues his solemn yet uplifting celebration of survival in the face of failure - of dreamers, lepers, refugees and pioneers 'curious and sad for all that is broken', as 'Retreat' recalls. Here are visionaries betrayed by their misplaced faith, 'the terrible spark of discovery': the Gospel parable lamp which would have cost a labourer his annual pay, Pliny's gods who 'do not walk amongst us now', or the scholarly, dried-up classicist wasting years on a single word of Sappho ('all that effort for "leather dildo" '), the unshaken belief of Antigone or Perpetua bringing only martyrdom and death, 'a turned field of stray bodies'. And yet, like all good poetry, Ashcroft pulls hope and triumph from despair: 'though the oil that feeds it/is spent' the gospel lamp still

burns. Meanwhile the desiccated, solitary scholar finds his own salvation:
And at night,
to all of his neighbours' distress,
there was raucous laughter, a lucrative trade
in foreign drink, and high and clear
his broken singing
('Translator')

But while *Dreaming of Still Water* shares many thematic concerns with its predecessor, it also represents an exciting progression, more assured, more confident, more mysterious; private moments of epiphany, quivering just out of reach on the horizon's edge, even more intensified:
finding their forgotten beauty
strange, like eyeless smiles.

('Runaway')

Elegant and compassionate, this is poetry of integrity, quiet, restrained, classical in the best possible sense, illuminating new approaches to the art of translation in all its varied meanings. Like the ancient Athenian currency in 'Coin Case' poetry of truly 'adult character', for those who understand that if we don't always learn from our mistakes we still need to revisit them; who can see the fragility of existence, the failure waiting to ambush us just around the corner, but keep on going anyway. Poetry, as Ashcroft's version of Cavafy's 'Two Men' attests, 'learning the pleasantries/of custom and culture, the language, the art'.

Cavafy also appears in *The Trees*, one of the many ghosts who haunt Peter Boyle's incandescent translation of acclaimed Venezuelan poet Eugenio Montejo, alongside Pessoa, Rembrandt, Hamlet, Orpheus, as well as the poet's own father and brother. But despite being featured in the Oscar-nominated film *21 Grams*, as well as winning the prestigious 2004 International Octavio Paz Prize for Poetry (and being nominated for the translation section of the up-coming Australian NSW Premiers Awards), the collection has so far been shamefully overlooked in British literary review pages. It is a great shame because everything about Salt's edition is a joy - from the introductions by both Boyle and critic Miguel Gomes to an illuminating selection of Montejo's prose pieces and a comprehensive bibliography, to the high quality design and production, not to mention the beauty of Boyle's measured versions: 'in the aroma we see old faces,' notes 'Talking Across the Table', 'once more alive'.

The quality throughout is such that you know almost as soon as you pick it up that this volume, like Jonathan Griffin's Pessoa or Nathaniel Tarn's Neruda, will become an old friend. As in Ashcroft's verse, Montejo's poetry looks to the past to unlock the complexities of the present: 'It's the green heat that joins them to me', records 'My Ancestors', 'I am the fields where they are buried'. Again, Montejo sees the failure at the heart of human endeavour, addressing, as Boyle notes in his illuminating translator's introduction, 'without shame the experiences of ageing, of loss, of disappointment…of disinterested love…' Yet poetry transcends such sadness, answering Montejo's question, 'How to get down from the web of formalities to the emotional nakedness of the world?':

Arriving from a great distance at any hour,
it gives no warning.
It holds the key to the door.
As it enters it stops to gaze about at us.
Later it will open its hand and give us
a flower or a pebble, something secret
but so intense the heart beats
too fast. And we wake.

('Poetry')

Like all good translations these versions have the feel and stature of an original; poems of beauty and loss, the wonder in the everyday - a thrush singing in a tree, a rooster's crow, the 'earthdom' of things, as Boyle translates Motejo's neologism *terredad*. This is deeply spiritual poetry for agnostic sensibilities, poetry written, Montejo notes in 'Fragments', as 'a prayer spoken to a God who only exists while the prayer lasts'. For here is a volume, both in original and translation, that understands the sacrament of poetry, the power - and fragility - of the thought once expressed, of the word spoken: 'The bird you hear singing is in Greek,' Montejo warns in his version of Cavafy's 'Ithaca' 'Don't translate it'. We can only be grateful that Boyle ignored this advice, to the immeasurable benefit of us all.

Josephine Balmer

Nikos Karouzos
Collected Poems
translated by Philip Ramp,
Shoestring Press (318pp., £12.95. ISBN 1-899549-95-1)

WHILE cultural achievement in modern Greece might always be overshadowed by its classical heritage, the renown of poets like C.P. Cavafy, or the two Nobel laureates George Seferis and Odysseus Elytis has helped to adjust perceptions of Greek soil as one of irretrievably past greatness. History, however, can repeat itself: one feels that an apparent fixation on these poets' laurels, while understandable, in turn deprives other major figures of the attention they deserve. Nikos D. Karouzos (1926-1990), whom readers of *MPT* have caught a glimpse of in the David Ricks-edited Greece Special Issue of 1996, is such a case; though his relative non-attendance in translation also has to do with Greek criticism only recently mobilizing (mainly in two symposia held at Athens University in the previous decade) to assert his significance. Here is a visionary poet of a truly unique and complex voice, astounding in its reach, enunciating both the profound and the self-evident in ingenious ways. And so the arrival, in Philip Ramp's translation, of the hefty volume (over 300 pages) of his *Collected Poems* owes much to this reassessment. Ranging from the *Poems* of 1961 to 1991's *Discoveries in Blue Cobalt*, appearing a year after the poet's death, it is published by John Lucas's Shoestring Press, which, backed by a number of Greek cultural bodies, has amassed in a short space a considerable catalogue of significant Greek poets - most notably Manolis Anagnostakis - till now conspicuous by their absence.

As could be expected from someone originally intending to be a philosopher, Karouzos's poetry is conceptually dense, following ideas across history and culture as they collide and interweave, always boiling down to one word. For Karouzos the poet has 'outstanding business with existence' and I cannot think of many that have approached from so many fronts its many facets, zealously dissecting its intensities and reflective paradoxes in view of the terrible voids beyond. Surveying the dead-ends of existential desolation, it is at the world-shaping order of art that Karouzos consistently pauses, meditating on its staying power. His poems, many offering themselves as 'music' or 'triptychs', gravitate towards a host of figures (Plotinus, Bach, Modigliani, Rimbaud, Marx) as they bear witness to the transubstantiations of life and person into art.

Keen as he is to find poetry in ideas and fuse both together in his own work, Karouzos never lets his eyes off the terrifying 'schizophrenia of language', the reality that builds both the noetic and poetic and is in turn created anew in truly great poetry. It is the rare self-identities in this intricate symbiosis that Karouzos is after, all too knowing that they can neither be approached nor conveyed easily; hence the often capitalized 'big' words, linguistic gymnastics and surrealist overtures in x-raying the imagery of mental states, of poetry that, for all its oral urgency, can appear cryptic and cerebral. One can see perhaps why both the critical unravelling of his *oeuvre,* as well as its translation, have taken their time.
Time, this 'skeleton without bones', is another reality of constant concern. It grants Karouzos some of his most incisive and essential lines as he shifts through its alchemies with awareness, lamenting the moments passing ('History of course/is not waiting for us/at the trolley stop'), summoning us to the seams when split seconds overlap with the historical, become personal myths.

In his mature work, recurring fragments and lists, like drafts of what could never have been, resemble a sort of inverse Ecclesiastes for a disjointed consciousness. With the austerity and parity of distilled understanding, precise aphorisms and phrases of stunning clarity ('the world is immortal because it dies so much'; 'I and time devour each other') remind us how we arrived at the timelessness of proverbs in the first place. Given the conviction with which they are stacked, it is not without significance that the language of numbers should increasingly partake in his. In 'The

Lethal Formulation' it is enough to just note, 'Life > Poetry / Life < Poetry /Offer yourself to non-endeavor.'

Philip Ramp approaches a truly daunting task with admirable eagerness and insight. Though his choice of words will miss the mark every now and then, and sometimes he exacerbates Karouzos's already knotty syntax, he successfully relays the essence and nuances of this multifaceted poetry in a language that, after all, does not have as an immediate access to its historical layers as Greek does. One often witnesses here what happens when the translator is also a poet and can be, in the space of a line even, both appreciative of the fragility of the verbal construct and forceful enough to have their version work as poetry. Results can be highly pleasing as in 'Dross of Immortality', a poem from the posthumous collection that perfectly summarizes Karouzos as he bids us farewell:

I always climb toward horror with greased boots,
       famished now by flames
             fluently secular
                   fluently in tears
       eternal choreographer of my diction
             and unquestioned jasmine.
Badly spent illumination in mauve and other dullness,
             ignoble horizon,
barking the creed of the dog, or an unbecoming
             hallucinatory Universe,
pharaonic queen through mathematical piety.
       I am what's involuntary of existence
my blend is not that of a flower, it is rawness,
       I am disposed toward a thousand years even though I fall
             eternally on bloody seconds;
       the winds have pointed me out.

Paschalis Nikolaou

Jan Twardowski *Serious Angel: A Selection of Poems* translated from the Polish by Sarah Lawson and Malgorzata Koraszewska (Waxwing Series No 3).
Dedalus (32pp ISBN 1904556175)

A Fine Line *New Poetry from Eastern and Central Europe* edited by Jean Boase-Beier, Alexandra Büchler and Fiona Sampson
Arc (270pp ISBN 1900072971)

THESE two collections stipple out the 'fine line' of cultural territory in

Central and Eastern Europe whose nation-states have just joined the EU. This is the stated aim of the Arc volume, with selections from Estonia in the North, via Latvia, Lithuania, Poland, the Czech Republic, Slovakia, Slovenia, Hungary and Romania, to Bulgaria in the South. I write 'stipple out' rather than 'draw': Arc presents two poets from each country, usually one man and one woman, neither over the age of forty. Dedalus' volume adds another point to the Polish section of the line: a selection of translations by Jan Twardowski, a retired priest.

Twardowski's is a poetry of real-world spirituality: quizzical, humane, accessible whilst staying the right side of trite (though sometimes only just):

He wrote 'my God' but crossed out because he thought after all
it's only *my* if I am selfish
he wrote 'God of humanity' but bit his tongue because he remembered
the angels and stones looking like rabbits in the snow
finally he wrote 'God'. Nothing more.
Still he wrote too much

The translations read beautifully. To some theoreticians (such as Lawrence Venuti), this is a bad sign: a translation that reads fluently, that is not spiky with the presence of the foreign, is an act of violation by the target culture. As a poetry translator, I could not disagree more. My ideal (unattainable though it may be) is to get a translation to a level where it sounds like an English poem, whereas stylistic spikiness can all too often read like translationese. In any case, the lack of spikiness in Lawson and Koraszewska's translations, the effortless flow of their English lines, allows the poetry's foreignness to get through. All good poetry, even that originally written in the reader's own language and culture, has foreignness - a newness of content, of voice, of viewpoint. Here, the foreignness is the voice of the old Christian sage who, like Hopkins in aim but unlike him in style, distils the spirituality out of the everyday. The Dedalus edition is monolingual, implying that the translations should be judged simply in their own right. But a check against the originals shows them also to be accurate in content and tone. Not that this came as a surprise: often, I find, the poems that read best in English are also the most faithful to their source.

As for Arc's arc, the editors and publishers should be congratulated on the scope and ambition of their grand idea - on the book's geographic range and the number of different poets and translators who have contributed. Though this might have resulted in a bag of bits, there is a surprising unity of theme, probably because of the selection criteria that were applied. The picture is one of a post-Communist, post-modern, post-everything world imbued, not by Twardowski's presence of God, but by the absence of grand idea, be it spiritual or political, leaving only the world which we see and inhabit. There are some striking exceptions, of course. Slovakia's Katarina Kucbelová, for example, is not post-modern but uncompromisingly modernist. The best of her poems have a crystalline beauty where language is more important than what it represents:

(*ideals:*)

;perfect - more perfect;
;almost perfect - perfect;

two: (from; to) (*movement*)

deceptively double: deceptively one

:unendingly approximating:

a perfect ideal needs a perfect ideal

By giving source and translated texts on facing pages, the editors invite comparisons. Thus James Sutherland-Smith and Katerina Sutherland-Smithová's versions capture lightness of Kucbelová's sound-structure well (zdanlivo dvojité: zdanlivo jedno   deceptively double: deceptively one).

Not all of Arc's poets and translators impressed me quite as much, I must admit. Though all seemed competent, only now and again did I sense a major poetic voice, and not every translator gave their poet the zing they deserved. This is perhaps the inevitable downside of the editors' ambitious and praiseworthy vision: they were, I suspect, often dependent on which poets their informants recommended, and on which translators could actually work from the lesser-read languages in this volume.

One major poetic voice, to my hearing, is Hungary's Krisztina Toth. Interestingly, she was also the only poet to use clear metric and rhyme forms, though this does not always come across in translation:

A hold neonja hullik	The moon's neon light falls
kilobbant ég a hóra	a flare of sky in the snow.
Átfordul, visszaperceg.	Turning, ticking, switching back.
Ébrenlét, homlokóra.	Wakefulness, brow of the hour.

Peter Sherwood's English misses the driving seven-syllable rhythm of the original, with its ironic reference to the certainties of Hungarian poetic tradition. One might argue, of course, that syllabic rhythms are 'un-English', but Sherwood does not use an accentual equivalent (trimeter, say) either. He does, however, compensate with a much stronger assonance-structure than in the original - though some might accuse him of over-domestication here, replacing Toth's deadpan rhythm-driven verse with a more mainstream Anglo-modernist lushness ('falls / a flare of sky in the snow' for the original Hungarian's 'falls / flickers out burns on the snow'). But I am quibbling here: overall, Sherwood's verse convinces.

Interestingly, whether the translators in this volume were source- or target-language natives seemed to have little to do with quality of poetic output. The best, like Ana Jelnikar (working from what I presume is her native Slovenian), did their poets justice, subtly adjusting what needs adjusting whilst leaving intact what is best translated straight - as in this poem by Primo☐ Cucnik:

Prva pesem govori o starem nacinu	First song speaks of the old way
☐ivljenja. Kako so bile stvari postavljene	of life. How things were set
v zacetku in kako se je vedelo, kje naj bi	in the beginning and how it was clear
	where
se koncale, ali v obrisih ponovo zacele	they should end or outlined begin
	again
z znamimi custvi.	with familiar feelings.

And doing justice is what translating is all about.

Buy these books. *Serious Angel*, for a deservedly popular poet, exquisitely translated. And *A Fine Line* for the inclusive verve of its cultural vision.

Francis Jones

Further Books Received

Agenda Vol. 40 No.4 Translation as Metamorphosis: Translations, Versions, Poems, Essays, Reviews edited by Patricia McCarthy, Agenda and Editions Charitable Trust, £12, ISSN 0002-0796
A fascinating and indispensable edition of the august literary journal, covering every aspect of literary translation - a must!

Dirk van Bastelaere, *The Last to Leave: Selected Poems*, translated from the Flemish by Willem Groenewegen, John Irons & Francis R. Jones, Shearsman Books, £9.95, ISBN 0-907562-70-1

Daemon 3 Exile/Mërgimtari, Survivors' Press, £2 (including spoken word CD)

Michel Deguy, *Recumbents: Poems* (with 'How to Name' by Jacques Derrida), translated by Wilson Baldridge, Wesleyan University Press, $19.95, ISBN 0-8195-6747-7

Claude Esteban, *A Smile Between The Stones*, translated from the French by John Montague, Agenda Editions, £7.99, ISBN 0-902400-74-6

Basim Furat, *Here and There: Poems*, edited by Mark Pirie, translated from the Arabic by various, HeadworX Publishers, ISBN 0-476-00885-9

Adel Karasholi & Dragica Rajcic, *Mother Tongues: Poems*, translated by Suhayl Saadi and Christopher Whyte, Goethe-Institut Glasgow/Scottish Poetry Library, ISBN 0-9532235-4

Ileana Malancioiu/Eilèan Ní Chuilleanáin, *After the Raising of Lazarus*, Southword Editions, £8, ISBN 1-905002-04-1

Desmond O'Grady, *Kurdish Poems of Love and Liberty*, Agenda Editions, £9.99, ISBN 0-902400-75-4

Moisés Castillo Florián, *Reflecting on Reflections and Other Poems*, translated by the author with Alison Dent, Anaconda Editions, ISBN 1-901990-02-8

Jacques Prévert, *Selected Poems*, translated by Sarah Lawson, Hearing Eye, £8.95, ISBN 1-870841-96-4

Books for review should be sent to Josephine Balmer, Reviews Editor, *Modern Poetry in Translation*, East Meon, St John's Road, Crowborough, East Sussex, TN6 1RW

Acknowledgements

We are grateful to the following:

Ruth Borthwick and the South Bank Centre for permission to use some of the versions of Akhmatova done for Poetry International in October 2004, and for their help in the preparation of our Akhmatova pages here;

Gallimard for permission to reprint Raymond Queneau's 'La Pendule' (copyright rests with Editions Gallimard, Paris) and to publish a version of it by Terence Dooley entitled 'Brother Blues';

Heinz Bachmann and Isolde Moser for permission to publish the translation by Mike Lyons of Ingeborg Bachmann's 'Kriegstagebuch'; her poems 'Bibliotheken', 'Wartesaal', 'William Turner', 'Der Gastfreund' and 'Jakobs Ring', together with translations of them by Patrick Drysdale and Mike Lyons.

Notes on Contributors

Josephine Balmer's recent books include *Chasing Catullus: Poems, Translations and Transgressions* and *Catullus:Poems of Love and Hate* (both Bloodaxe, 2004). She is currently chair of the Translators' Association and also Reviews Editor of Modern Poetry in Translation.

Paul Batchelor is writing a Ph.D. on Barry MacSweeney's poetry, at Newcastle University. His versions of Ovid were published in *MPT* 3/2 (Diaspora).

Ruth Borthwick is Head of Literature & Talks at the South Bank Centre in London.

Colette Bryce was born in Derry in 1970 and has lived in England, Spain and Scotland. Her second collection *The Full Indian Rope Trick* is published by Picador.

Terence Cave is Emeritus Professor of French Literature in the University of Oxford and Emeritus Research Fellow of St John's College, Oxford. He is the author of a number of academic studies, in particular on French Renaissance literature and cultural history. His translations include Mme de Lafayette's *The Princesse de Clèves* (Oxford World's Classics, 1992) and two stories in *Wonder Tales*, edited by Marina Warner (London, Chatto & Windus, 1994).

Belinda Cooke was born in Reading in 1957. After her English/Russian degree she went on to complete a Ph.D. on Robert Lowell's interest in Osip Mandelstam. Her poems and translations have been widely published in various journals and anthologies, including *Cyphers, The Shop, Agenda, Acumen, Poetry Salzburg* and *Shearsman*. She is currently completing a selection of Marina Tsvetaeva's poetry. Her translations of Viacheslav Ivanov's Roman Sonnets appeared in *MPT* 10.

Terence Dooley has started late as poet and translator. His published career as the latter began with a well-meant hoax, his versions of three Vera Pavlova poems in *MPT* co-credited to his sister Maura (a Willy and Colette arrangement). Worse, a poem has just appeared in *Soundings* under his name which is really by W.G. Sebald. He has edited his mother-in-law Penelope Fitzgerald's collected essays (*A House of Air*, 2003) and is preparing an edition of her selected letters and poems to be published by Fourth Estate.

Patrick Drysdale read English at Oxford and taught English and Introductory Linguistics at Memorial University of Newfoundland. He subsequently worked as a lexicographer and editor of English language and literature textbooks for a Toronto publisher. He returned to England in 1982, runs a small estate, and writes poetry.

Sasha Dugdale is a consultant and translator for the Royal Court Theatre. Her first collection *Notebook* was published by Carcanet/ Oxford Poets in 2003; her second is due out in 2007. Her translations of Tatiana Shcherbina, *Life Without: Selected Poetry and Prose*, were published by Bloodaxe in 2004.

Elaine Feinstein is a prize-winning poet, novelist and biographer. She was made a Fellow of the Royal Society of Literature in 1980, was given an honorary doctorate in 1990, and has served as Chairman of the Judges for the T.S.Eliot Award. Her work has been translated into many languages. Her biography, *Ted Hughes: The Life of a Poet*, came out in 2001, and *Anna of All the Russias , a Life of Anna Akhmatova* in June 2005.

John Greening (b.1954)'s most recent collection is *The Home Key* (Shoestring, 2003). Earlier volumes have included a *Selected Poems* and *The Tutankhamun Variations* (Bloodaxe, 1991). He has won both the Bridport Prize and the TLS Centenary Prize for his poetry. His guide to the poets of the First World War appeared last year. His play about Lindbergh was premiered in the USA in 2002. He is a regular reviewer for the *TLS*.

Marilyn Hacker is the author of twelve books of poems, most recently *Desesperanto* (W.W. Norton, 2003) and the translator of five collections of poems, including Vénus Khoury-Ghata's *She Says* (Graywolf Press, 2003) and Claire Malroux's *Birds and Bison* (Sheep Meadow Press, 2004) . She lives in New York and Paris.

Paul Howard is a Scholar of Balliol College, Oxford, reading French and Italian. His first translation of a G. G. Belli sonnet won joint second prize in the 2004 Times Stephen Spender Prize for Poetry in Translation. He was recently Fellow in Residence, Hawthornden Castle International Retreat for Writers.

Kathleen Jamie's poetry collections include *The Tree House* (Picador 2004), which won the Forward Prize, and *Jizzen* (Picador 1999) which won the Geoffey Faber Memorial Award. Kathleen is a part-time lecturer in Creative Writing at St Andrews University.

Francis R. Jones has published 11 books of translated poetry from Bosnian-Croatian-Serbian, Dutch, Hungarian and Russian. He is Senior Lecturer in Applied Linguistics at Newcastle University.

Sarah Lawson (b. 1943 in Indianapolis) is a poet and translator, mainly from French and Spanish, and **Malgorzata Koraszewska** (b. 1943 in Uzbekistan) is a translator of non-fiction from English to Polish. Together they have translated the poetry of Jan Twardowski from Polish, published in earlier volumes of *MPT* and in a collection, *Serious Angel* (Dublin: Dedalus Press, 2003).

Karen Leeder is Reader in German at New College, Oxford. She has published widely on German poetry: including *The New German Poetry* due out in 2005. She also translates from German, including most recently: Raoul Schrott, *The Desert of Lop* (Macmillan 2004), and Evelyn Schlag, *Selected Poems* (Carcanet 2004).

Mike Lyons served in Army Intelligence in post-war Austria, then studied German at Edinburgh University. As a teacher he became a Head of Modern Languages, subsequently teaching at Oxford Brookes University and Ruskin College. Felix Mitterer's verse monologue *Sibirien* had its UK premiere in a translation by him and Patrick Drysdale.

Richard McKane is a poet and translator who has been translating Russian and Turkish poetry since the sixties, publishing widely with Anvil and Bloodaxe among others. He is most noted for his collections of Anna Akhmatova, Osip Mandelstam, Nazim Hikmet and Oktay Rifat.

He also works as an interpreter for Victims of Torture in London. He is a regular contributor to *MPT*.

Paschalis Nikolaou has an Onassis Foundation scholarship at the University of East Anglia where he is completing a doctoral thesis on the interface of literary translation, creativity and autobiography. He is currently working on translations of the poets Richard Burns and Nasos Vayenas.

Neil Philip has published two collections of poetry, *Holding the World Together* and *The Cardinal Directions*. His work has appeared in various Japanese literary magazines, including *Literary Space*, *The Subaru Monthly*, and *Poetry and Thought*. His 'linked quatrains', exchanged with Kijima Hajime and his circle, have been published in three dual-language collections.

Sean O'Brien's fifth book of poems, *Downriver*, won the Forward Prize. *Cousin Coat: Selected Poems 1976-2001* appeared in 2002. His version of the *Inferno* is to be published in 2006 by Picador. His plays include a new verse version of Aristophanes' *The Birds* (National Theatre) and *Keepers of the Flame* (RSC/Live Theatre), published by Methuen. His critical book *The Deregulated Muse: Essays on Contemporary Poetry in Britain and Ireland* was published in 1998 by Bloodaxe. He lives in Newcastle upon Tyne and is Professor of Poetry at Sheffield Hallam University.

Cecilia Rossi originally from Buenos Aires, now lives in Norwich where she is completing a Ph.D. in Literary Translation at the University of East Anglia. She holds an MA in Creative Writing from Cardiff University; her poetry and translations have been published in various journals, including *New Welsh Review, Poetry Wales, Point of Contact (Syracuse University)*, as well as anthologised in *The Pterodactyl's Wing* (Parthian Books), edited by Richard Gwyn.

Jo Shapcott is the author of four books of poetry. Winner of Forward and Commonwealth prizes, she is currently visiting Professor at the University of Newcastle.

George Szirtes's *Reel*, was the winner of this year's TS Eliot Prize for poetry. He translates poetry and fiction, mostly from his mother-tongue Hungarian into his foster-mother tongue English. His translations have won the European Poetry Translation Prize and other awards.

Cristina Viti's versions of Apollinaire and Cendrars appeared in *MPT* no. 16. Current work includes a new translation of the poetry of Dino Campana, research on other Italian poets, and readings at various venues.

Antony Wood is a translator of Pushkin and publisher of Angel Books, an imprint devoted entirely to translations of classic foreign authors.

Subscription Rates (including postage by surface mail)

	UK	Overseas
Single Issue	£11	£13 / US$ 24
One year subscription (2 issues)	£22	£26 / US$ 48
Two year subscription (4 issues)	£40	£48 / US$ 88

Student Discount	UK	Overseas
Single Isssue	£8	£10 / US$ 18.50
One year subscription (2 issues)	£16	£20 / US$ 37
Two year subscription (4 issues)	£28	£36 / US$ 66

Standing Order Discount (UK only)	
Annual subscription (2 issues)	£20
Student rate for annual subscription (2 issues)*	£14

To subscribe, please write with your name, address and postcode to: The Administrator, Modern Poetry in Translation, The Queen's College, Oxford, OX1 4AW, UK or e-mail administrator@mptmagazine.com Please indicate your payment method, and which issue you wish to start your subscription with. If you are a student please indicate how many more years you plan to take to complete your studies. Thank you.

Payment Methods

Cheques: Cheques should be made payable to Modern Poetry in Translation (Sterling, US Dollar or Euro cheques accepted)

Credit Card: To pay by credit card please visit www.mptmagazine.com

Standing Order: Please request a standing order form from: administrator@mptmagazine.com or write to the address above.

* Students must notify us when they finish their studies, and will then be liable for the full subscription rate.

Back issues

MODERN POETRY IN TRANSLATION. Series 3 Number 1

INTRODUCTIONS

Edited by David and Helen Constantine
Cover by Chris Hyde

Contents
Editorial David and Helen Constantine

Mahmoud Darwish *A State of Siege*, translated by Sarah Maguire and Sabry Hafez

Boris Ryzhy, nine poems, translated by Sasha Dugdale

Giorgio Caproni, 'Ligurian Suite', translated by Robert Hahn

Liam Ó Muirthile, five poems, translated by Bernard O'Donoghue

Eunice Odio, 'Ode to the Hudson', translated by Keith Ekiss and Mauricio Espinoza

Luciano Erba, eleven poems, translated by Peter Robinson

Philippe Jaccottet, from *Green Notebook*, translated by Helen and David Constantine

Jorge Yglesias, Two short essays and five poems, translated by Peter Bush

Gerhard Falkner, seven poems, translated by Richard Dove

'The Traveller' - A Tribute to Michael Hamburger, by Charlie Louth

Price £11
Available from www.mptmagazine.com

DIASPORA

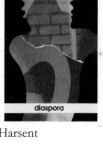

Edited by David and Helen Constantine
Cover by Lucy Wilkinson

Contents
Editorial   David and Helen Constantine

Carmen Bugan, an essay and two poems
Yannis Ritsos, fifteen *Tristichs*, translated by David Harsent
David Harsent, three poems from *Legion*
Goran Simic, an essay and four prose poems
Forough Farrokhzad, four poems, translated by Gholamreza Sami
Gorgan Roodi
Marzanna Bogumila Kielar, six poems, translated by Elzbieta Wójcik-
Leese
Lyubomor Nikolov, six poems, introduced by Clive Wilmer, translated
Miroslav Nikolov
Adel Guémar, four poems, translated by Tom Cheesman and John
Goodby
A note on Hafan Books by Tom Cheesman
Sándor Márai, 'Funeral Oration', translated by George Gömöri and Clive
Wilmer
Paul Batchelor, versions of Ovid's *Tristia*
Olivia McCannon, three poems
Yvonne Green, three poems
Ziba Karbassi, three poems, translated by Stephen Watts
Volker Braun, nine poems, translated by David Constantine
Wulf Kirsten, ten poems, translated by Stefan Kobler
Knut Ødegaard 'Taking out the Hives' translated by Kenneth Steven
Euginio Montale, three uncollected poems, translated by Simon Carnell
and Erica Segre

Reviews
Bernard Adams on George Szirtes's Agnes Nemes Nagy
Paschalis Nicolaou on David Connolly's Yannis Kondos
Will Stone on Antony Hasler's Georg Heym

Price £11
Available from www.mptmagazine.com